T0065271

A ROSE AT THE POOL

38 YEARS AND NOT A DAY LATER

MOTHER ROSE

authorHOUSE®

AuthorHouse™
1663 Liberty Drive
Bloomington, IN 47403
www.authorhouse.com
Phone: 1 (800) 839-8640

© *2015 Mother Rose DeSefano. All rights reserved.*

No part of this book may be reproduced, stored in a retrieval system, or transmitted by any means without the written permission of the author.

Published by AuthorHouse 09/02/2015

ISBN: 978-1-5049-4798-5 (sc)
ISBN: 978-1-5049-4797-8 (e)

Print information available on the last page.

Any people depicted in stock imagery provided by Thinkstock are models, and such images are being used for illustrative purposes only. Certain stock imagery © Thinkstock.

This book is printed on acid-free paper.

Because of the dynamic nature of the Internet, any web addresses or links contained in this book may have changed since publication and may no longer be valid. The views expressed in this work are solely those of the author and do not necessarily reflect the views of the publisher, and the publisher hereby disclaims any responsibility for them.

KJV
Scripture quotations marked KJV are from the Holy Bible, King James Version (Authorized Version). First published in 1611. Quoted from the KJV Classic Reference Bible, Copyright © 1983 by The Zondervan Corporation.

NJB
Scripture quotations marked NJB are from The New Jerusalem Bible, copyright © 1985 by Darton, Longman & Todd, Ltd. and Doubleday, a division of Random House, Inc. Reprinted by Permission.

ABOUT THE AUTHOR

Many women in ministry or in religious circles have suffer with many of the same experiences I had to endure as a child, a young adult, and as an abused spouse having to raise two children alone. The Church has been a great source of support for me and my family. I experienced the occult, religious discrimination and misinterpretation. I hope that my experiences help someone else.

ACKNOWLEDGMENTS

Let me begin my acknowledgements by dedicating this book to my two children, Camille and Tommy, not because of its content, but because of what I refer to as 38years of waiting; and during those 38 years, I put my children through hardship, personal misfortune, and pain, both physical and psychological. I want to personally apologize to them for what I believe was a lack of consideration on my part that cheated them out of a certain level of family life. I'm sure that the both of them would say that the apology is not needed, but my spirit says differently.

I want to thank my Bishop and General Overseer, Bishop Leroy C. E. Newman, who encouraged me to write this book, my children, Camille and Tommy, my grandchildren, and members of my church for helping in the smallest way with the completion of this project: Brittney, Shamekya, Cerise, First Lady Tameka, and Mother Moore for proofreading and providing the resources for the final draft.

I want to finally acknowledge my cousin bobby because it was he who saw the light of God in me while I lay waiting at my pool of Bethesda.

38 YEARS AT THE POOL

AND NOT A MINUTE MORE

I started to write this book a while back in September 2012, but every time I started to write about a circumstance or an event that occurred in my life it would leave me down hearted. I knew there had to be a reason for writing this book more than just for the sake of telling the story of my life; so I waited on the Lord and looked to the hills from which comes my help to get the understanding and the purpose for the book. If this book helps just one person I can look back with joy and fulfillment of divine purpose.

From the age of twelve I clearly remember the guidance of my grandmother Rose, (my father's mother) because my mom seemed to be at work most of the time. We lived in an apartment upstairs from her. I was kept busy with chores which I really enjoyed doing. Among my many duties was scrubbing three flights of stairs and hallways, sweeping the front stoop and sidewalk, cleaning out the chicken coops in the back yard, and collecting the eggs.

I loved my grandmother and felt very close to her; she was really the only companion I had during those years. I loved my mother too, but I never really had much time with her because of her work schedule. When she came home, she cooked and did her own chores around the house. She would be exhausted, it would be late and time for bed. My chores were somewhat routine and centered around minor house duties, the backyard, and of course doing my homework before going to bed, usually before my mother got home.

Our bathroom was a long room outside of the apartment, 2 steps to go down and it consisted only of a toilet. In those days we had no bathtub; we bathed mostly in the kitchen sink or in a basin. No matter how tired my mother was, she always took care of cleaning the bathroom. When I got older I walked to the public bathhouse where there were bathtubs and showers. These were common in most communities, but we had to carry our own soap and towels. Actually, I enjoyed going to the bathhouse because it gave me a chance to leave the house and tour the neighborhood. The only other time I was allowed out of the house alone was to go to church or school.

On one particular Saturday, my mother really looked tired. I wanted to surprise her by cleaning the bathroom myself while she went to the store. That day everything seemed fine; I took a bucket of water, mop and soap down the two stairs and started mopping. I took off my shoes so I wouldn't ruin them. Barefooted, I started cleaning. I must have put too much soap on the floor because it was very slippery and I fell backwards onto the two steps. There was a nail that I had never noticed before probably because it wasn't on the top of the step but on the side sticking out of the front of one of the steps. As I fell, my head struck the nail, I was so frighten that I laid there bleeding until my mother found me. Shocked and nervous I was taken to the emergency room where I received three stitches. After a while I recovered and continued my daily routine of cleaning and doing my homework.

Although my chores kept me busy and while I basically enjoyed them, there was one thing I hated doing, and that was going outside to wait for the vegetable man to pass by with his horse and buggy. I wasn't waiting because my grandmother wanted to buy vegetables but because I had to sit on the curb with a scooper and a pail, so that whenever the horse came by and dropped his manure (dung) I would scoop it up for my grandmother to spread around in her garden as fertilizer. I always hoped that the children in the neighborhood wouldn't be out playing so that I would not be seen doing this. They would look at me as someone strange, especially because I never came out to play with them.

During the summer my grandmother and I always took a trip to Manhattan; these trips were always exciting. Every Tuesday morning we would visit St. Frances Assisi, during the time of "Novena." Novena (from Latin: Novem, meaning Nine) is an institutional act of religious devotion in the Roman Catholic Church, often consisting of private or public prayers repeated for nine successive days in the belief of obtaining special intercessory graces.

It is believed that a specific request made during Novena Prayer would be answered after nine weeks. The prayers were prayed to St. Lucy. I remember seeing a stature of a woman holding a plate with 2 eyes on it. I asked my grandmother about it and she told me that St. Lucy was the patron saint of the eyes, and if anyone had an eye problem, the Novena Prayer was to be made to her. My grandmother never said if her prayers were ever answered, but I do know what Paul said in Acts 17:29.

> *"Therefore since we are God's offspring, we should not think that the divine being is like gold or silver or stone--an image made by man's design and skill.*
>
> *NIV*

> *Forasmuch then as we are the offspring of God, we ought not to think that the Godhead is like unto gold, or silver, or stone, graven by art and man's device*
>
> *KJV*

From a child I have always loved going to church and asked my grandmother if we could go more often. She said since I would soon have to go for lessons in order to get what was called "First Holy Communion," that I could start going on Sundays at our local church. In the Catholic faith, you could not receive communion without "religious instructions." I was allowed to go to Sunday mass alone although no one else in my family went. The only rule was I had to go to the 7 a.m. service, because we always went to dig for clams on Sunday. We would dig most of the day and collect bushels and bushels of them. My grandmother, a young widow with eight children ranging from ages eight to eighteen, (my father was the oldest), had a way of providing any way she could for the family. My father worked in a picture frame factory; it was there that he met my mother.

We had to get to the beach early in the morning to dig for the clams while the tides were still low. When the tides were going to be high early, I was not allowed to go to church in order for us to get to the beach earlier before they came in. We could not get clams during high tides. I would not dig for clams because I had a fear of drowning; I felt if I drowned I would go to hell, and I was taught in my Catechism class that missing church on Sunday was a "mortal sin" that had to be confessed in a "Confession Box." This had to be done before I could receive communion. We were taught that there are two kinds of sins, Mortal and Venial. Mortal sin had to be confessed to the priest and he would give you "penance" to say the day before you were to receive communion. This usually consisted of saying the Lord's Prayer about 10 times and the "Hail Mary" Prayer about 10 times. However, the Priest would always decide the number of times. Venial sin was considered a lesser sin where we were simply told to tell God we were sorry. I know now what Paul said to the church at Rome:

> *There is therefore now no condemnation to them which are in Christ Jesus, who walk not after the flesh, but after the Spirit.*
>
> *Romans 8:1 NIV*

I know today that my saying the Lord's Prayer the way I did and my prayers to Mary were to no avail. After I came to Christ, I was reminded of how I used to hurry through the Lord's Prayer in order to get home quickly. Yes, there was no time for humility.

One Sunday, after I had gotten over my fear of drowning, my mother and I were digging for clams with the family. We decided to swim across the bay because the clams were more plentiful that day on the other side. I would swim across the bay, put clams in my bathing suit, and swim back to where my grandmother was and put them in the basket. I had done this time and time again, in fact so many times that toward the end of the day I was very tired. I came up with the idea that, if I filled my bathing suit with as many clams as it would hold, I would save time and trips, so I filled my swimsuit with clams and started to swim back. As soon as my feet left the ocean's floor I started to sink because the clams were so heavy they weighed me down. I could not come up. Thank God my mother saw what was happening and jumped into the bay and ripped the bathing suit off with her bare hands, causing the clams all to fall out; with that I started to come up again.

The angel of the LORD encamps around those who fear him, and he delivers them.
Psalm 34:7 NIV

Sin, like the clams in my bathing suit is weighing so many believers down who were afloat at one season in their lives. But only by the grace of God, He wants them to heed to His call, and like the over loaded swimsuit I was wearing, they are starting to sink. God creates situations in our lives that will force us to go in a direction that we should have chosen ourselves.

You may have concluded by now that my grandmother was the matriarchate of the family and found a way by any means necessary to take care of her household. Digging and selling clams was limited to the summer months on Mondays and Tuesdays and only if necessary other days of the week. It was my job to deliver the clams to the neighbors for twenty-five cents per dozen. During the fall we made wine in the basement. There was a large vat with a large rotating wheel where grapes would be pressed. The wine making was not an easy task, but we took turns pushing the wheel in a circular motion as we walked around the vat. At the beginning of the process it was very easy, but as more and more grapes crushed, it would take two people to turn the wheel; so one of my uncles who was about seventeen years old at the time would always volunteer to help me. He would bring me down to the basement and always put me in front of him to push the wheel. As he pushed he would say that the wheel was hard to push then he would force himself against me as hard as he could. He didn't just push with his arms, but he used his whole body. I didn't know then what he was doing. We were not told, as children are today to look out for these kinds of behaviors. I could feel every part of him against me. I asked him to just push with his arms but he said if he did the wheel would not turn. As bad as it may seem, it could have been worse. God was watching over me even then when I really didn't know Him as I do now. I am reminded of what God said to Jeremiah.

Before I formed thee in the belly I knew thee; and before thou camest forth out of the womb I sanctified thee, nd I ordained thee a prophet unto the nations.
Jeremiah 1:5 KJV

Times were hard, we were in the middle of World War II and my grandmother was always looking for a way to make a few extra dollars. At that time nylons were hard to come by because nylon was being used to make parachutes for the soldiers. As I forestated, my grandmother and I would go by subway to Manhattan in the summer months for the festival of Novena. For some reason I always looked forward to going there for church. I believe that was where my love for church began. Directly across the street from the church were two well know department stores where my grandmother would buy two or three dozen pairs of lady's hosiery, and during the week I would go out through the neighborhood selling them.

I don't ever remember seeing a Bible as a child, neither in my home nor in the church. Whatever doctrine I was taught, I must have learned it from my grandmother or during Sunday morning mass, and what I learned I believed it to be true.

> *Then you will know the truth, and the truth will set you free."*
> *John 8:32 NIV*

God has been preparing me for this day ever since I was a child in spite of what I would call today my grandmother's "not so holy doings." You see my grandmother also ran a "numbers game" in the neighborhood. On Thursdays and Fridays I would go to all the neighbors to collect sheets of paper with numbers to play on them, along with their money. I would bring them home and on Saturday I would go back to everyone with the winning numbers and the winning money if any. I always hoped they would win because they would always give me a quarter if they did. Of course, if anyone had won a large amount they would have to go personally to my house to collect their winnings from my grandmother.

Although there were other children on the block, I only got to know them at school or to say hello if I passed them while going to the store for my mother or grandmother. I was not allowed to play with them or invite them over, but I never was lonely or idle.

> *I will not leave you as orphans; I will come to you.*
> *John 14:18 NIV*

There was always something that I had to do. There was also a little old lady who rented a room from us for whom I was responsible to go visit every day, and ask if she needed anything. She would occasionally send me to the grocery store to buy fifteen cents worth of American cheese. I was always happy when she sent me for the cheese because she would always give me two pennies for myself. I still remember her name, "Mrs. McEroy." She always sat in a large club chair…I never saw her out of it.

The most vivid memories I have of solitude or being alone are the times when my grandmother would send me out into the backyard with an orange. I would sit, peel and eat the orange. After eating the orange I would take a pail of water and rinse off a few radishes that I had plucked from the garden and eat them; then I would amuse myself by balancing a light weighted flat stick on the steps with half of it sticking out. I would then put a pebble on one end and pretend that I was a storeowner; the stick would be my scale. I would sprinkle dirt on the other end, pretending it was coffee; when the stick tilted that was one pound of coffee. I guess I was picking up my grandma's business mind.

Another one of my memorable responsibilities was to go once or twice a week, to the vegetable store around the block and get vegetable trimming for the chickens to eat, mostly outer lettuce leaves. By the way, the owner was also one of my grandmother's numbers customers. He would take the outer leaves of each head of lettuce and put them into a crate and I would bring them home. We had a chicken coop in the backyard and every morning I would go and bring in the eggs. I remember a special day when on my way home I met one of the girls who was about my age sitting on her stoop next door to my house. She asked if I would come out to play; I told her I would ask my grandmother. I was quite excited about it and was sure she would say yes after I fed the chickens. But her answer was a firm no. There was to be no exchange of friendship with other children.

I believe this was the first time I felt rebellion in my heart. My anger was too much to hold back, so I took my anger out at the only thing I could. I decided it was the fault of the chickens. After I fed them, I raised up the crate and flung it into the coop, hitting one chicken, killing it. All I could think of at the time was a commandment I had heard in church, "Thou shall not kill." Needless to say I rushed over to the "confession booth" that

Saturday and told the Priest I committed murder. He asked me, how did you do it? After I explained, he told me to say "10 Our Fathers" and "10 Hail Mary's." He didn't know who I was because the "confession booth" is closed in. He asked about my parents coming to church but I told him my parents don't go to church. I now know that the killing of the chicken was not a condemnable sin, but the good thing about redemption is that God Himself redeems us of our sins.

> *The LORD will perfect that which concerneth me: thy mercy, O LORD, endureth for ever: forsake not the works of thine own hands.*
>
> *Psalm 138:8*

The next day in church during his sermon he spoke of a little girl in confession yesterday whose parents do not attend mass. I remember trying to slide down in the pew hoping no one would know it was I. I was so relieved of my "mortal sin" being taken away by confession and receiving communion. I say "mortal" because as I forestated, we were taught there are two types of sin...Mortal and Venial. "Mortal" being those that you must confess to a priest in order to receive communion. "Venial" sins you did not have to go to confession but just tell God you're sorry.

I was also very relieved about my mortal sin being taken away that I no longer cared about seeing other children. I buried myself in my chores, going to church on Sundays, and doing schoolwork. I liked going to school because, at least, I got to see and be with other kids. After school I would have to go directly home and set the table for dinner every night. My mom always cooked dinner the night before. When she came home from work and after dinner I would wash the dishes and scrub the stove. This was very important to me because I always thought my mother to be ragged and tired.

We didn't have a washing machine, so on Saturday I would watch my mother scrub all the clothes on a washboard over the sink. I remember feeling bad and my heart seeming to sink every time she took out the washboard. I don't think it was the scrubbing of the clothes that hurt me so badly. It was the combination of her having to bend over, and in silence I could hear her swearing. She had no one to complain to but herself. I have not mentioned my father, until now. You see, throughout my childhood, my father never said much and when he did, it was to give an order. At dinner we were to eat and not speak. We were not allowed to eat our meal unless we ate bread first. I remember one night telling my father I did not want the bread. Remembering what I had been taught in my catechism class, I told him, "Man does not live by bread alone." That was all that made sense to me at the age of eleven. Needless to say, my father flared up in anger at me and insisted that I eat everything. Most of our meals consisted of spaghetti and one night I felt very sick to my stomach. I told my father I didn't feel well and couldn't eat the spaghetti. He told me I could not leave the table unless I ate it. Well, my mother was never allowed to say anything contradictory to my father in these situations so I forced myself to eat the spaghetti. Afterwards, I left the table and went to my room. I thought if I just could lie down a while I would feel better; but suddenly, I vomited everything up all over the floor. For that reason, I don't like spaghetti and red sauce even today.

> *Better is a dish of vegetables where love is Than a fattened ox served with hatred.*
> *Proverbs 15:17ASB*

The only immediate family to whom I was exposed were my parents, my grandmother from my father's side, two younger brothers and my father's brothers and sisters. Although my brothers were younger than I, they were given more liberties. They were allowed to sit on the stoop. At the age of ten to eleven they also suffered the same silent treatment as we all did from my father. I always believed and still do today that my father was a bitter man. I believe he blamed me for being born at the changing of his life. My birth caused him to have to take on the roll of father. He could not continue doing the things he was doing, it seemed that I was the blame for his failed expectations. As the pressure of parenting grew harder, someone had to be blamed; I thought it to be me. I don't know what kind of childhood my father had because he never spoke of it. My mother sometimes spoke of her parents and her sisters and brothers, but I was never allowed to see them, even though they all lived a few blocks away. Whenever they were mentioned, my father and my grandmother would speak evil of them. My grandmother would tell me that my maternal grandmother was known all around town to have a bad reputation for owing everybody, and that she bought her groceries on credit and sometimes was not able to keep up with her payments because she gambled on horses and played the numbers. She also told me that my maternal grandmother stayed up nights until early mornings playing poker. I guess my paternal grandmother felt that she was better than my maternal grandmother and more justified because she didn't play numbers; she was only a number writer. Even at the age of eleven, I knew that one was as bad as the other; therefore, I could not understand her reasoning.

> *And why behold you the speck that is in your brother's eye, but consider not the beam*
> *that is in your own eye?*
> *Matthew 7:3 KJV*

I can clearly remember my grandmother being involved in witchcraft. She had a book – no not the Bible, it was some kind of dream book. Neighbors would come to our house with problems, my grandmother would refer to this book to solve them or give meaning to their dreams. The book had the "answers" to all your dreams. She also used a deck of cards to advise people in their dilemma. On New Year's Eve, people would come to our house for several reasons: one to learn a special prayer that my grandmother said could only be taught on New Year's and to be healed from excruciating headache. Those who had these headaches were told that they had been given the "evil eye," meaning someone had placed a curse on them that caused the headache. They were told that there was a prayer that could be prayed that would rid them of the curse; my grandmother would pray privately to remove the curse. Anyone wanting to be taught the prayer was told that it could only be told to them on New Year's Eve. If it were taught any other time there would be an even greater curse placed upon them. I "kind-a" thought that there was a connection between being raised in an occult environment and going to a church with a lot of ritualism and no Bible teaching. I feared my father greatly and had confusing and mixed feelings about his authority in the house. I couldn't understand how he could be the head of the house but allowed his mother to set the rules of the house while at the same time operate in the occult.

But when he, the Spirit of truth, comes, he will guide you into all the truth. He will not speak on his own; he will speak only what he hears, and he will tell you what is yet to come.

John 16:13 NIV

My father did discipline in our house. I remember there was a leather strap over the kitchen stove in my grandmother's downstairs apartment. My father's two younger brothers, unmarried, were still living with my grandmother and whenever they did wrong in her eyes she would tell my father and he would beat them severely. When I heard him beating them it made me cringe. As an added part of their punishment, my grandmother would send them to the basement to continue with the wine making. I was always told to go down and help wherever I could. It was there where both uncles would inappropriately force themselves on me. Until that time I had respected them very much; they were about seventeen and eighteen at the time. I feared saying anything because the strap was a symbol of chastisement and I knew that if I said anything I would be the one who did wrong and my father would use that strap on me. I was only about eight years old; therefore, I convinced myself that it was all right because all three of us were victims of the strap. I was very little and at that age there was very little communication exchanged between my father and me. I seem to remember there being a "silent fear," but in spite of everything, I had a great admiration for him and was confident that as a father he would protect me.

One day at the age of twelve my father came home from work with a small package specifically for me. I was so excited and shocked. I couldn't wait to see what it was. He had never done anything like that before, neither for my brothers nor, as far as I know, for my mother. When I opened and looked in the package, it was a pack of blank writing paper. He said I could use it for school if I wanted to. I was so happy and thrilled about the paper. I cherished it highly because my father thought of me; it made my household duties seem joyful. I now remember Paul's writings to the Ephesians 5:10

try to discern what is pleasing to the Lord

Ephesians 5:10 ESV

A few days later my mom was out with my two younger brothers, and I was scrubbing the kitchen stove when my father walked in. I turned and said good evening to him, as we were trained to always greet him and my grandmother. But this time he hesitated awhile and gave me a compliment on how I looked. I had never heard him do this before. I was elated to say the least. I guess I thought that between the gift of paper and the compliment, my father was having a change of heart about family relations and I was determined to do nothing to anger him. I would do whatever it took to please him and to make my mother and brothers' lives more at peace. As usual my father would go out until about mid-night to play cards, and of course to drink wine.

I had been harboring the secret of my two uncles inappropriately molesting me at the age of eight, now at the age of twelve I am blindside by my own father coming into my room. The first time I was awakened in the middle of the night to see my father hovering over me, telling me everything would be alright and not to be afraid. He assured me this was just between him and me and no one else would understand, not even my mother. It was to be our little secret; he then left the room. The next day I was confused but assured that my father really loved me. At dinner he was exceptionally polite, yet he was very silent. The next night he went out again and again returned about midnight, this time I wasn't sleeping. I couldn't sleep wondering what was going to happen next. As I lay there dreading, sure enough he came back into the room and told me again, "It would be alright, he would never do anything to hurt me." He then began to fondle my breast and remark as to how much of a woman I was becoming. When he left the room I told myself, "I must tell my mother," but when I thought of the pain it would cause her, I could not bear to tell her. I had already seen enough of her pain and sorrow, and I would not be responsible for her going through any more pain. From then on I begin avoiding him during the day, as best as I could, but at night he still came to my room, I would tell him to leave because it was not right. He said to me, more or less, when I am ready he will be there. This was to be the beginning of years of fear and uncertainty.

> *For the mind that is set on the flesh is hostile to God, for it does not submit to God's law; indeed, it cannot.*
>
> *Romans 8:7 ESV*

A few months after my first encounter with my father, he decided to open a candy store around the corner from where we lived. My grandmother, needless to say, helped him financially. The store would be open from 6 a.m. to 11 p.m. and my mother left her job to work in the store. My father would open the store at 6 a.m., and my mother would arrive at about 1 p.m. so that my father could go home and take a nap. I was ordered to come straight to the store after school and work with my mother. My father would come back to the store in the evening so that my mother could go back home to do her chores; I was to stay and help my father until somewhere between 7 to 8 o'clock. I also had to be there on Saturdays and Sundays in the winter, since there was no clamming. During the summer when school was out I had to be there every day. As oddly as it may seem, I loved being at the store. I liked making fountain sodas, ice cream cones, frappes, and ice cream sodas for the customers. I enjoyed selling newspapers and listening to the jukebox; people would come in and put quarters in the jukebox to hear their favorite hits. It seemed that the lemon ices in the hot summer were the best. We also had a frankfurter stand where we would sell hotdogs for twenty cents each.

As much as I liked working at the store, it became a dungeon of fear. The store had a backroom where you could rest when the opportunity presented itself. It was in that room where my father would go when we were there alone and call me to molest me. He would just lean me up against the wall and expose himself; he would even penetrate between my thighs and kiss me on the lips. This went on for 2 years. As humiliating as it was there was absolutely no way that I wanted my mother to know; so like the man at the pool of Bethesda, I waited for my deliverance.

Be of good courage, and he shall strengthen your heart, all ye that hope in the LORD.
Psalm 31:24 KJV

When I became fourteen years of age, I graduated junior school. My grandmother, a seamstress, along with her two daughters had the last say as to what kind of school I would attend. I really didn't want to be a seamstress and it seemed that my mother was not allowed to help me choose. This didn't bother me so much because I would be out of the house and on my own and happy spending my days in school, meeting new friends and experiencing new ways to face the challenges of life. I started to see how easy it was for other children to be happy and engage in innocent conversation with each other. I first took notice of the difference between their personalities and my own. They were more extroverted, while I was definitely a loner and more introverted. They were so carefree and fun loving, they just enjoyed clean fun. I, on the other hand, trusted nothing or no one. It seemed I was always suspicious of them, even when they just wanted to play a game. I knew then that what my father had done to me was reflected in my character and the relationship I was developing with my new friends and classmates. I always knew it was wrong and that it had to end regardless of the consequences. Now that I'm writing this memoir, I see something in my circumstance for the first time that I never saw before. I hear the voice of God say to me that the pack of paper my father gave me was a passageway to years of molestation. As I look back, prophetically, it has led to my writing this book and hopefully to the lighting of someone's burden who has gone through the same thing for so long, and is living with the burden. I hope that it will lead someone to Christ and bring him or her to know that a Savior is waiting to heal them and give purpose to their lives.

Let us not be like the man at the pool of Bethesda, waiting 38 years for someone to come along to recognize his circumstance. I'm here to tell you that there may not be a physical cure for your problem, but I know there is a spiritual answer to every situation.

"Take up your bed and walk." John 5:8

That same year, at fourteen, after realizing that I was somewhat different from my new friends and classmates; I took a walk to the nearest police station. The officer asked me to sit at the desk and tell him why I was there. I spoke in a low voice and told him I would like to have my father arrested. He asked me what he had done. That's when I started to stutter and cry. I asked if he could arrest him if I did not say what he did. There was absolutely no way I wanted my mother to know. The officer told me, "No, I cannot do that." I am sure he had an idea because he kept me there trying to get me to talk. I finally left and told him I would come back another time. His eyes were sad and piercing, I knew he sensed a wrong. At that moment I decided to tell my mother. I blurted out 2 years of lost innocence. I never thought I could ever imagine or know the pain she must have felt but years later, which I will speak of later on in this book, I found myself walking in her shoes.

My mother went downstairs to my grandmother's apartment. I could hear her as she screamed everything out to her. My grandmother refused to believe it, but said she would talk to my father. When she spoke to him I was not allowed to be there, but I heard screaming and yelling from upstairs. I never had to face my father concerning this matter, and he never approached me in a sexual way again. For the next 4 years that followed, I would compare my life to living in a prison.

Shall mortal man be more just than God? shall a man be more pure than his maker?
Job 4:17

As for my mom, I learned in my teenage years that she had developed spinal meningitis at about the age of two. The doctors had given up all hope for her survival but the Lord saw fit to let her live physically. As a result of the attack she was left with her eyes damaged and crossed. In school she was not allowed to take sewing or to hold a needle in her hand. She could not take part in strenuous eye programs. The illness also affected her mentally. What I noticed mostly was her inability to function in activities that we take for granted such as balancing a checkbook. For instance, she opened a checking account at a local bank, but would constantly be over drawing because she could not understand how to deduct each check. Finally, we were able to convince her to close the account and pay only by money orders.

I remember when a store opened called Times Square Store. They put up a sign that read "TSS." I asked my mother one day, where she was going, she said, "to "Tis" meaning "TSS." To her that was the name of the store. I tried to explain to her that the actual name of the store was Times Square Store. And that TSS was the abbreviation, but to her it made absolutely no sense. She insisted TSS was pronounced just that way (Tis). There was the time she went on a Weight Watcher diet. She came home with a tiny scale and said she was allowed 2oz. of cheese only. She brought cheese and started putting it on the scale. When the scale reached 2oz. she realized that she had one slice left over in her hand. Not knowing what to do with it and not being one to waste food, she decided to eat it. I am not trying to joke about this. I just want to explain that there was a limit to her worldly understanding, her inability to understand things you and I take for granted. But I will never forget the day my mother made a statement that sparkled like a radiant star of wisdom and insight. I could only say, *"Thanks be to God for his indescribable gift!"* 2 Corinthians 9:15

My mother's father passed away and as I sat next to her in the funeral home, she cried hysterically, calling out my grandfather's name. The sadness of her crying whispered throughout the hall, so I simply said to my mother, "Ma, stop." To my surprise, almost immediately she said, "alright, I'll stop." At that moment you could have blown me over with a feather. How could she have stopped so suddenly? It wasn't until weeks after the funeral, when we were talking about my grandfather that I reminded her of the incident. I asked her, "how, while being so emotionally wrought, could you just stop crying because I asked you to?" Her answer blew me away. She said, "Because I realized what I was doing to you."

I told you that my father had stopped talking to me. Well, for the next four years, not only would my father not speak a word to me, but also neither did my grandmother. To add insult to anger, more than ever, I was not allowed to speak in the house, not even to utter a word. It was as though they disowned me.

> *Be strong and of a good courage, fear not, nor be afraid of them: for the LORD thy*
> *God, he it is that doth go with thee; he will not fail thee, nor forsake thee.*
> *Deuteronomy 31:6 KJV*

During the day I had to work in the candy store. My father would not bother me there anymore, but it was clear that I was not to say a word to him. When I stayed home to do my chores, I liked to listen to music on the radio. The moment he came home, I would say good evening, as I had been taught from a young child, but he would never respond, instead he would go straight to the radio and shut it off. This went on for four years. In spite of the distance that developed between my grandmother and me because of what happened between my father and me, I loved her very much; this also added to the misery of those years. As far as my mother was concerned, even though she did not hurt me as my father and grandmother did, ever so often there was a conflict between us that I could not reason with.

In my last year of high school, I was enrolled in the work-study program. I was assigned a part-time job in Manhattan in a sewing factory. It was a curriculum requirement for graduation. We worked alternating weeks (one week in school and one week at work), and were paid weekly. My father, although he was not speaking to me, told my mother that my pay envelope was to be put on the refrigerator without being opened. For four years any communication from my father to me was through my mother. After leaving the pay envelope on the refrigerator, the next day my mother would give me enough money to ride back and forth on the subway for the week, not a penny more. Lunch was to be taken from the house. If I needed shoes or something else, my mother would tell him and he would give her the money to buy them. I really believe that as far as my father was concerned, I was dead to him. There were a few times in high school when we would have half days. I would take advantage of them by going to the library instead of going home because my father knew nothing about the half days. I enjoyed going there and browsing through the books.

Around the age of sixteen, I started to grow more curious about my mother's parents and siblings who lived a few blocks away. By this time my situation at home had made me begin to feel more and more angry and rebellious toward my father and grandmother. I was angry because I thought it was wrong for my father's family to look down on my mother's family, and for me not really knowing why. So I decided to start going to see them whenever I could steal away for an hour or two. Whenever there was a half-day at school, I would spend time at my other grandmother's house. By doing so, I saw a totally opposite side of what I had been told. My grandmother (Carmella) was so different.

When I came over she would usually have a pack of cigarettes on the kitchen table while she was preparing dinner. She would stop for a minute, sit and talk with me while enjoying her cigarettes. If she had time, she would watch television. She loved opera, usually performed in Spanish. She was able to translate the entire opera word for word perfectly. Her knowledge of the words in songs never ceased to amaze me.

> *There is no fear in love; but perfect love casteth out fear: because fear hath torment.*
> *He that feareth is not made perfect in love*
>
> 1 John 4:18

I found myself going there for at least an hour every day after school and then rushing home to do my chores before my father found out. There came a time when my father no longer wanted me in the store during the week. He now had my younger brother come in to work. I only had to go on Saturdays, and as soon as I got there he would leave to go home. I would be left there to work alone. I was ever so grateful when he would leave because not only did he not say anything to me, he also would not answer me if I asked him anything. His leaving eliminated a lot of heaviness. I would work till about 7 or 8 p.m. He would always come back to the store to close and he would just say to me "you can go now."

I remember one day going to see Grandma Carmella. She wasn't feeling very well and when I asked her what was wrong, told me that she had been up all night and had only two hours of sleep. She played poker all night until early morning. My grandfather was a gentle and hard-working man who always spoke softly, but this time I heard him arguing with Grandma Carmella. I eventually found out that Grandma Carmella was addicted to gambling. She not only gambled with cards but also played the numbers and bet on horses. Every bookmaker in town knew her and treated her politely. Since most of her money went to gambling and horse racing, she owed every grocer and butcher in town. She could always get groceries on credit because somehow she made sure that everybody was paid, especially the bookmakers. In spite of Grandma Carmella's habits, I found myself drawn to her. All I know is that she showed me love and affection.

> *Above all, love each other deeply, because love covers over a multitude of sins.*
> *1 Peter 4:8*

I was now sixteen and a victim of peer pressure. I remember the first time I asked someone in school for a cigarette; they gave it to me and I put it in my pocket. When I got to my grandmother's house, she wasn't home, so I lit the cigarette and just as I finished smoking it, I heard her coming up the stairs. I flushed the cigarette down the toilet. When she walked in the door she asked me if I had been smoking. I told her no because I was petrified, thinking that she would tell my father or Grandma Rose. To my surprise she held me in her arms and told me, "This is a secret between me and you." Then she assured me she would tell no one. At the same time she advised me not to smoke again at least till I was an adult. Needless to say, I didn't smoke again until I was eighteen.

With all my Grandmother Carmella's weaknesses I sensed in her a wealth of worldly wisdom, not so much the wisdom of God, but surely the love that God said we should have. It was all the wisdom she had gained down through the year, perhaps from her mother and from life experiences, considering that I never saw a Bible in the house. I had a great respect for her and started to realize the difference between her and Grandma Rose. I didn't mention that there was also an aunt and an uncle living there with Grandma Carmella. My uncle was not married and worked the night shift at the post office. He would get up every afternoon about one o'clock, and I would make every effort to get there to see him before he left for work.

Grandma Carmella was usually out and I looked forward to making breakfast for him, then sitting and listening to his conversations. He, in my mind was the most intelligent person I had ever met. Talking to him was like having a conversation with Mr. Einstein himself, but more importantly I could sit alone with him and never have a fear of him saying or doing anything that would hurt me. In fact, some of our conversations were of the innocence and purity of a girl my age. I never told him about my experiences with my father and two uncles. He was such a protective uncle, I know had I said anything to him of those incidents; he would not have hesitated to go to my father.

As I grew older, living at home became increasingly worse and I knew I could no longer remain there. I was eighteen and wanted to be on my own. Ideally, I would have loved to stay with Grandma Carmella. I was ready to graduate and was looking forward to working in a factory full time. I also felt I could contribute to Grandma Carmella financial crisis. But the thought of what my father would have put my mother through made me shudder. It was a situation like the Hatfields and McCoys. They would not have reacted in a positive manner to my leaving to be on my own with my mother's family. In fact, I think they would have preferred that I live anywhere, as long as I didn't live with Grandma Carmella. That's how bitter the resentment was. I became eighteen in January and was determined to get my diploma the coming June.

I had an uncle who lived in Elmont so when I graduated I told him about my plans. He told me I was not to leave home not knowing where I was going, so he made arrangements for me to stay with him and his wife who was my mother's sister until I found a place. Not soon after, I packed a few clothes and left a letter on my dresser for my mother telling her I was sorry but there was no other recourse. I assured her that I had a job and a place to stay and that there was no need to worry. I did not write in the letter where I was going, fearing my father would find it.

When I settled in at my aunt's house I called the candy store to speak to my mother, at a time that I knew my father wouldn't be there. She felt better when she heard I was living with her sister. I got a job sewing at a factory where my uncle worked. He would take me to work every morning with him in Brooklyn. He worked long hours; therefore, I had to work long hours also because I had no other way of getting home from Brooklyn to Elmont. I didn't mind because I had developed a hard working state of mind and way of life.

Out of my salary, I made arrangements to pay my aunt and uncle rent expenses; however, after two weeks my uncle told me he had finally found me a furnished room through a friend he trusted dearly. The furnished room was about a half block away from another sewing factory where I was able to get a job sewing. That week I called my mom again to tell her I needed clothes to wear because I had left almost everything home. We made arrangements to take the subway and meet at Union Square and 14th street in Manhattan. As I waited in the station, I saw her coming with a big shopping bag in her hands. I think that's the first time I realized that my mother would not leave my father. I was her daughter but I realized she was concerned about her two younger sons at home who were ten and fourteen years old.

At one point I told her we could all live together somewhere else and I would work two jobs to care for all of us. For reasons of her own she couldn't go that far. She returned home and I went back to my furnished room. From then on I continued to work, live on Yankee Doodles for lunch and 15-cent pea soup and milk for dinner (which I loved). During the summer, after work I would sometime go home, have a Yankee Doodle and a glass of milk, and take a shower because the room was very hot. I would take a walk through the neighborhood. I loved to walk. One night I guess I walked a little too far, and about 10 pm I found myself in Highland Park walking around the reservoir. I was actually enjoying myself when suddenly approaching me were five teenage boys. They started a conversation and I found myself willingly talking to them. Perhaps, it was because I had no one to talk to. They were friendly enough, so I thought, but after 5 minute they sort of huddled in a corner speaking in a low voice. Afterwards they all started walking towards me at the same time. Instinctively I became aware of the danger. I don't remember if or to whom I prayed but in my distress I saw one boy stop and turn to the others and say, "no." He then came over to me and told me to leave now and go home. Thinking of Jesus, our Savior, who met the man at the pool, I realize that not only did he just show up at the pool where the man had laid for 38 years, he will also just show up today, even if you don't know Him or did not call Him just like He showed up at the reservoir. That was the last time I was ever in Highland Park.

> *For he will command his angels concerning you to guard you in all your ways;*
> *Psalm 91:11 NIV*

I continued working, and spending my Saturdays window-shopping. I cannot explain to you why I did not go to church on Sundays; truthfully, I do not know why. Perhaps, it was because I just saw the church as a building and never thought of it as an answer to my problems. Now that

I know Christ, I understand that as long as people attend church because of the glory of the building, they will find nothing, but if they see it as a place where one can meet God, it could become not only a place of worship but also a hospital for sinners and not a museum for saints.

As July approached, I thought of my mother's birthday that was coming up. Suddenly I was over whelmed with the thought of her being alone on her birthday. I decided I must go back home for her sake. I was determined to not be undermined, but I had to go back to make sure she wasn't being mistreated and looked down upon because I had left home. I was determined to see that she was absolutely not being blamed because she had a "wayward daughter." You can tell from the tone of my voice that I had become more independent since I left home. I called her at the candy store and told her I would be coming back. I assured her that it would be all right if my father refused to talk to me. I would continue working in a factory and in the candy store if necessary. I was sure that I would not have to face the abuse anymore, because it was now in the open.

> *Wherein ye greatly rejoice, though now for a season, if need be, ye are in heaviness through manifold temptations:*
> *1 Peter 1:6 KJV*

I went back home on my mom's birthday. She must have told him I was coming because he did not look surprised to see me there. But from that day on he never said one word to me. Whenever I was home cleaning or cooking a meal and he happened to walk in, he always would immediately walk over to the radio and shut it off. Whenever I was in his presence, no matter where it was, home or at the candy store, there had to be absolute silence. When I would greet him as he entered a room, he continued not to acknowledge or look at me.

After returning home and while working in the candy store, I was making a cup of coffee for a customer who was also from the neighborhood who knew us well. My father was sitting quietly at the counter, but suddenly in an unexpected and angry voice said to the man, "Do you know this whore was out of the house for 2 months?" I was embarrassed but I refused to leave the store. The man looked at my father in a consoling manner then he looked at me in, what I felt, was a contemptible and judgmental manner. I didn't really care because I was determined that first of all, it was none of his business and secondly, I was not going to leave my mother alone again. I had become more offensive at this time, just waiting for that man or anyone else to blame my mother for what I had done. I was eighteen years old and working. It was the second job I had since I left home. I could not help but think of what Paul said to Timothy that they will speak lies in hypocrisy, having their conscience seared with a hot iron (1 Timothy 4:2).

I had become friendly with a girl my age who told me about a young fellow who lived in her neighborhood who she knew because both their families came from Austria. She thought it would be nice for me to meet him. I told her she could give him my Grandmother Carmella's phone number because we never had a phone at our house. She did and I made arrangements to be there when he called, on certain evenings.

After we talked on the phone for a while we decided to go on a "blind date." I told him he would have to pick me up at my house because I thought that that was the way it should be. He came over a few nights later and met my mom and my two brothers who were ten and fourteen at the time. I told him that he would first have to go to the candy store to be introduced to my father; when we got there, I introduced him. Let call him "Syl, this was not his name. He put his hand out to shake my father's hand and said, "hello Mr. DeStefano," my father rejected his handshake and said, "The name is Jerry." We left there and went on to see a movie. I apologized for my father and just said he is a very strict man. We continued to date, but my father set the rules. I was to be home no later than 10 o'clock. It was not easy because Syl could not get to my house until 7:30. We would try to catch a movie or even visit one of my mother's relatives, but because he lived in Jamaica, NY and I lived in Brooklyn; we would mostly just go back and forth visiting relatives.

He then introduced me to his parents who lived in Jamaica. I detected that his father was very strict, but was a sincere man. His mother always seemed cold toward me and I eventually found out the reason.

After dating for six months, Syl asked me to marry him; I loved him and wanted to marry too. When I told my mother, it seemed that she was never so happy; not only was she elated but her entire side of the family was also. I suppose I thought at the time this was God's way to bring peace. My mother's family knew once I married, I would not be under my father's dictatorship.

We planned to marry within the next six months. Knowing that a wedding would be costly, I asked my father if he would permit me to just pay a share of my living expenses so that I could save for the wedding, the gown and the reception; he told me "no"! I would have to continue to give him my paychecks. Troubled by my father's attitude, we went to tell my future mother-in-law of our plans; she became very sullen and irate. I asked her if we had done anything wrong and she told me she always dreamed of her son marrying a girl from her country. Wouldn't it be sad if God held back salvation because of our nationality? But God has no respect of person, (Romans 2:11).

That night as Syl was taking me home he decided we should stop in a bar for drinks. I told him that his mother was upset and perhaps we should reconsider what to do. He said something that ight that I never forgot, "if my mother were to die tonight, I wouldn't even cry."

I felt we both were living unfortunate lives. I knew that he wouldn't have said this if that was all there was to it. I found out later that there were other things bothering him that he was keeping inside. Had I known Jesus at the time as I know Him now, I could have tapped into a source of power that would have helped the both of us. But instead we carried our burdens with us for the next six months while we continued with the engagement. During this time we obeyed all the rules of both households. My father was speaking to neither Syl nor me.

One night as we were driving home we had a flat tire; I panicked because I had to be home by 10 pm. If I wasn't home by ten, I knew what my father would do. We finally fixed the flat and I managed to make it to my house at 10:15 p.m. When I put my key in the door it wouldn't open because my father had put the double lock on the inside. I was too afraid to ring the bell knowing what to expect. My aunt who lived in the basement had her window open, so I climbed in and fell asleep on the couch.

In the meantime Syl was spending more and more time in bars. I also noticed whenever we were at his parent's house when he had coffee, he would always put a little whiskey in the cup. I asked him why did he do that and he said that it was the tradition of their country. He also had two uncles who when they came over did the same thing. When they went home they were usually very intoxicated. I started to blame Syl's drunken behavior on his mother's motherly controlling ways. I was determined that once Syl and I were married there would be no more need for Syl to get drunk. I was convinced we would have a good life together. What was wrong with that picture? I was trusting in the arms of the flesh.

> *Trust in the LORD with all your heart and do not lean on your own understanding.*
> *In all your ways acknowledge Him, And He will make your paths straight*
> *Proverbs 3:5-6*

As the wedding date approached, we went to visit Syl's close buddy, a childhood friend, who lived in Manhattan. This friend was married and had 3 children and had fallen on hard times. We went to visit them and found them sitting on crate boxes for chairs with no food whatsoever to eat. We scraped up 100 dollars and gave it to him. His friend started to cry and told us that he would re-pay the money as soon as possible.

We started to make arrangements for the wedding only to be told by my father we couldn't be in charge of the wedding. My father and his mother would take care of everything. I reminded my father of all the money I should have accumulated to use for the wedding arrangements. He said that the money was all gone. I asked him how could that be since I hadn't used any of it. He told me if I didn't like it, the wedding would be called off. I had no choice but to have him run the wedding as he wanted to. Even my mother had no say; she couldn't even go with me to choose my gown and I knew that that was one of her biggest dream.

Choosing the gown was the job of my godmother, my father sister. She was as stern as my grandmother and father, but she had a quiet spirit, and was always nice to me. There were two gowns in the bridal store; one was one hundred dollars and the other was one hundred twenty-five dollars. I fell in love with the hundred twenty-five dollar gown, but my aunt said simply, there was not enough money to get it. So I had to settle for the cheaper one. At one point while shopping with my aunt she tried to convince me that I was getting married too early. The next problem was the choosing of the maid of honor. My father's mother said that someone from Syl's family would be the maid of honor. I told her I didn't know anyone in Syl's family that well, and I wanted to have my mother's sister as my maid of honor. My father once again threatened to call off the wedding, and once again I had to give in to his demands because he had all the money I had saved.

I decided to find a second job in order to get extra money for the wedding, and of course we would need our own apartment and furniture. I found another small sweater factory that was running a night shift. Syl was a construction worker and together we saved as much as we could. It wasn't long before I realized that Syl's mother and my grandma had entirely taken control of the wedding planning. They both were mean spirited and whatever they said was the law. My mother just went along with everything; all she wanted was for me to be happy. For her, to see me get married was the answer to much of her worry. In one way I could understand my grandma's meanness, perhaps it was because her son's sexual immorality was going to be exposed. However Syl's mother was a proud and selfish controlling woman of whom I had no clue as to why she was the way she was except that I was not Austrian. She had no daughters and Syl was her only son. Both she and her husband were so unbending with us that at one point we talked about eloping. But because my mother married after my conception I just couldn't have her hurt because of gossip and accusations. I decided I would stick it out as long as necessary.

Finally the day arrived and we were married at "Our Lady of Mount Carmel." The same church I received my first holy communion and confessed my "mortal sins." My mother and father's family all sat on one side and Syl's family sat on the other side. When I walked down the aisle with my father he did not so much as smile or grin. He would not even smile for pictures. After the ceremony, as we turned and started to walk up the aisle, Syl and I slowly headed towards my mother, as she leaned to embrace us, immediately my father's mother ran over and grab me and shoved me across the aisle to Syl's mother so that she would have the honor of being the first to be acknowledged. Afterward we had a small reception with family and friends. You could see in me, for a moment, a level of bitterness.

> *For I see that you are in the gall of bitterness and in the bond of iniquity."*
> *Acts 8:23 ESV*

The next day, we had about $500 in wedding gifts. I told Syl we should put most of it in the bank and just leave some to go away for a few days. We did just that and we went to Niagara Falls. When we came back, we moved into a two-room apartment that we had rented the month before. It consisted of a kitchen and living room. We had purchased a sofa bed to sleep on at night and to use in the living room during the day. We continued our routine working schedules. Sometimes at night my mother's family would come over to visit. I liked my work schedule (Monday to Friday). I did my chores and shopping on Saturdays and once in awhile I went to mass on Sundays.

One night my maternal grandmother stopped by and asked if she could borrow two dollars. I truly did not have any cash money on me. Because we wanted to one day buy a house we were in the habit of banking all we could. I felt horrible and guilty that I didn't have the two dollars to give her, and then I remembered that she had a habit of borrowing from any and every one she could in order to satisfy her gambling habit. I told myself that it was better for her that I didn't have two dollars. Paul warns us that we should not become stumbling block to the weak (1 Corinthians 8:9).

After four weeks of marriage, Syl told me he was going to go rabbit hunting that coming Saturday. I knew he was going with his father and his two uncles. I was told that they always did this even before he met me. That Saturday morning I got up at 3 a.m. because they would pick him up about

4:30 a.m. I was excited for him to go hunting and was looking forward to making a big breakfast and packing food for them to eat.

Afterward I cleaned up and went back to sleep for a few hours. Later during that day I took a walk to the candy store to spend some time with my mother. Afterward I went shopping for food to cook for dinner because Syl was due home about 4 p.m. Since we were still newlyweds, I was feeling romantically inclined to make a dinner with candlelight. I remember making a pasta dish and veal Parmigianino. That dinner still sticks out in my memory. Time started to escape. Four o'clock p.m. came and Syl was not home. I didn't think anything of it until 5 p.m. then 6 p.m. came and went, still no Syl. Since we didn't have a phone, I decided to go down to the public phone booth to call my mother-in-law to see if she had heard from them, fearing something grave had happened. My father-in-law answered the phone and said that they had been home since 4 p.m. and that they had dropped him off in front of the house. He did say Syl had been drinking with his uncles. My father-in-law was not a drinker but did not seem to mind them drinking. He assured me that he was probably all right and would be home soon.

About 8 p.m. Syl walked in totally intoxicated and belligerent. I decided to ignore him, thinking we would talk tomorrow. While he sat at the kitchen table screaming at me for not cooking any meat, I pointed to the platter that had the meat in it. He stood up from the kitchen table and started walking toward the living room. There was a glass door that separated the kitchen from the living room. As he came near the glass door he swung his hand into the door, cursing the name of his friend to whom he had loaned $100, saying, "he did not repay the loan."

He passed out on the floor covered with blood that was gushing from his wrist. I panicked and screamed. There was a tenant living upstairs from us who heard the screams; he ran down and immediately tied a tourniquet around his arm. He then managed to get him into his car and took us to the emergency room. I sat there waiting in total numbness and disbelief. Finally the doctor came out to see me and asked how much did he have to drink? My replay to him was, "my husband doesn't drink." The doctor, of course, knew I was in denial, but at nineteen years old I was not going to see my dreams disappear. I was told to go home that night and come see him the next day. Throughout the book I will refer to "the man at the pool because it is a "type" of my life and how long He waited for me to surrender.

I went home and returned the next day, Syl and I hugged and cried; he told me he was sorry for what had happened and promised that he would never drink again. Luke tells us to be merciful even as our Father is merciful. The doctor came in the room and said that Syl had cut a nerve and tendon, and that he would never have the normal use of that hand again. We had not told my in-laws yet, and Syl did not want them to know the truth. We decided that we would tell them that it was an accident. I told my mother-in-law that while he had gone hunting, I decided to wax the kitchen floor. Syl slipped on the floor and his hand went into the glass. Unexpectedly, she said it was my fault that her son could not work anymore at the construction site and she would never forgive me. Her domineering ways were showing their ugly side more and more. But it was okay. I didn't really care what she thought of me. I continued on my job while Syl was home recuperating. About 2 to 3 weeks later, I realize I had not gotten my menstrual yet. I thought it might have been from the stress. Syl and I walked over to the doctor's office and he examined me.

The doctor told me that he thought that I was pregnant but it was really too soon for him to be sure. He started to prepare a needle to give me an injection. I asked him what was the needle for; he told me if I was pregnant it was soon enough in the pregnancy that the injection would bring down my period. I told him that I had come there to find out why I was not menstruating; I did not come there to stop the pregnancy if I was pregnant. He asked me if the man sitting in the waiting area was my husband and I said yes. He asked why was my husband's arm in a sling. I told him his nerves and tendons were cut. His response was, "you do know that your husband will be out of work no less than a year." I said, "doctor, if I am pregnant, I know that it's not going to be easy during the days ahead, but I do know this, God is going to give me the most beautiful baby you have ever delivered." And with that we left the doctor's office and went home.

For so is the will of God, that with well doing ye may put to silence the ignorance of foolish men:

1 Peter 2:15

I continued to work at the factory, sewing, until two weeks before I gave birth. About a month before that my father-in-law somehow managed to have my husband work at Kennedy Airport, which was called International Airport at that time. Syl worked in the booth collecting tolls because he had minimal use and power in his hand. Since I worked days and he worked evenings we rarely saw each other.

During my pregnancy my father wanted nothing to do with me. On Saturdays when I didn't have to work I would spend time at my grandmother's house on my mother's side. We would sit and talk about the upcoming birth. In those days there was no test to tell if the baby would be a boy or girl, but my grandmother had her ways of knowing, so I was led to believe. She asked me what was my due date then she looked at the calendar and told me, according to the position of the moon, I was going to have a boy. My question was, does this mean everyone whose due to deliver on that day would have a boy. She assured me that this was a very personal thing. My mother's sister stopped by with her own remedy. She would dangle a needle and thread over my wrist; if it dangled in a circle it meant I would have a girl, if it dangled back and forth I would have a boy. Then there was the fortune-teller whose cards were to determine my future. She told me that the cards said Syl would never drink again. Well I heard her, but my concern was the influence that his mother had over him. Therefore, I told her that my problem was that his mother keeps contacting him telling him what to do. She told me that it didn't matter that his mother kept calling. She said, "she may be his mother, but you are his wife."

Thus saith the Lord GOD; Woe unto the foolish prophets, that follow their own spirit, and have seen nothing

Ezekiel 13:3

I didn't make much of an effort to see my paternal grandmother, mainly because every time I saw her she always reminded me of who the Godparents of the baby should be. So I tried to avoid her whenever possible. My maternal grandmother had a family recipe that she always made for Easter, but she would never give it to anyone. One day during my seventh month, I went to see her. She sat down at the table with me and said "RoRo" (I was called "RoRo" by the family), I would like you to sit and write this recipe for me; it's my secret recipe. I told her, "Grandma, I am not really interested at twenty years old in baking cakes." She said to me, "that's alright you don't have to make it now. I just want you to write it down and keep it." I agreed to do so. Two days before Easter grandma made the cake; two days later, my grandmother passed away from a massive heart attack. Her death was so traumatizing that I started bleeding and was rushed to the hospital. It was the first time I can remember praying fervently to God; up until then I just prayed. My concern was, if I had the baby after being married only eight months, my father's family would have accused me of being pregnant before marriage, and would point their fingers at my mother again. One of my uncles came to see me, my mom's brother. He said to me, "the baby would be alright even if born early." I said to him, "who would believe me." I never forgot his answer, "I would."

> *An hypocrite with his mouth destroyeth his neighbour: but through knowledge shall the just be delivered*
>
> *Proverbs 11:9*

Days passed and my pregnancy continued. I went every day to see my uncle and we tried to comfort each other during the weeks after my grandmother's passing. We would both cry and laugh remembering her ways. My mom would also go with me sometimes although my father didn't like it. It seemed that anything involving me was wrong in his eyes. At other times when I would go to visit my mom just to see how she was coping with the passing of my grandmother, I sensed that she was struggling with it. Also, she was not allowed to visit her own mother or even have her over to her house at any time. I was now in my ninth month, and I believed it was upsetting to my father that I had become so close with my mother's family. God knows I desired to be close to him and his family too, in spite of all that has happened. He was overwhelmed with anger and ordered me out of the house, in spite of my mother telling him to at least let me have something to eat or drink because it was sweltering hot outside. He refused, so I left. I walked back to my uncle's house where we sat in front of the window and just talked. I remember him saying that I looked somewhat worried. I told him that I was just wondering if I could be a good mother. His response was, "yes you will because you are concerned about it."

> *When my father and my mother forsake me, then the LORD will take me up.*
> *Psalm 27:10*

The day came for my baby to be born, the Lord blessed (my husband and me), with the most beautiful baby girl. I realized that I keep saying "me" instead of us, but by this time I was starting to get use to doing lots of things alone because my husband worked nights and slept all day. I was somewhat mother and father and was adjusting to it very well. Childbirth was by no means what I expected, even though the Lord brought my baby and me through. I had natural childbirth, and was in labor for 43 hours. I remember the doctor saying as the baby was being born, "I cannot do this" and he walked out of the delivery room for what seemed like hours, although I'm sure it was probably a few minutes. Another doctor came in to speak to me. He said, "Ma'am, the baby's head is out but the cord is twisted around the head and we won't be able to continue with this delivery." But God! Although the birth was not easy, God stepped in just in time. Yes, in spite of the dilemma, I had my baby naturally, and yes my baby is saved, sanctified and filled with the Holy Ghost and for the sake of this book we will call her Ms. C. During the delivery, I could hear the doctor say, "If we continue the baby could be strangled and die; so we are going to push the baby back inside of you and use forceps to turn the head upward so we can remove the cord more readily." Without any further warnings I suddenly felt the gash of a knife. I momentarily blanked out, but later I awakened to see my baby being held up and taken away as I was being stitched up. They told me later that I had received a lot of stitches. A few days later I developed an infection, which resulted in me staying in the hospital for two weeks. When I was ready to go home I was not able to sit or even lie on my back because the pain was unbearable.

During my recovery my mom would stop by for a short while, but she always had to rush back to the candy store. After a couple of weeks my mother-in-law sent word that I should stay at their house in Jamaica until

I got better. My mother-in-law was starting to lose her eyesight due to glaucoma but she assured me that my father-in-law would lend a hand after he came home from work. He usually got home at or about 11 p.m. and would be home until about 3 p.m. the next day. In the meantime, my husband was also working nights, but when he was home he would just watch TV during the day until it was time for him to leave for work. It seemed that he had become acclimated to that life style. Well, I suppose that I just thought it was a temporary circumstance. From 3 p.m. every day after my husband and father-in-law left, it was just the baby, my mother-in-law and I.

We would mostly talk about the baby and she sometimes brought up the subject of the baby's name. I explained to her that my husband and I had already discussed names for the baby and agreed that if it was a boy, he would choose the name and if it was a girl, I would choose the name. I told her I already had chosen the name, "Patricia," before my grandmother passed, but since then I changed my mind and now want to name her after my grandmother. My husband and I agreed and chose a form of grandma "Carmela's" name. We decided on "Ms. C." My mother-in-law seemingly was very angry, and told me that we had been disrespectful, and that she should have had a say in the matter of naming the child.

> *Therefore shall a man leave his father and his mother, and shall cleave unto his wife:*
> *and they shall be one flesh.*
>
> *Genesis 2:24*

After thinking about how my father's family had always named their children after their grandparents, I decided to do what, at that time, I perceived to be the right thing, even though inwardly it was breaking my heart. I told my mother-in-law, "Yes, mom you are right; I will name the baby after you." With that she answered, "No! I don't want the baby named after me." When I asked her what she meant, she told me she wanted the baby to be named after her mother. Well… with that, my inner man flared up, but I calmly informed her that that would not happen. I went on to let her know that since she was not obligating me to name the baby after her, "Sylvia," then the baby's name was to be ""'s n." At that, she turned, and in a furious rage, told me she would not call my baby by her name, not ever, even until the day she dies.

Actually, she did not call my baby by her name for almost 3 years. She would just call her sweetheart every time we would bring her to the house. Gradually after almost 3 years she did start calling her by her name. Getting back to the suggestion that I stay at her house to recuperate from the stitches received during birthing stage, after the discussion of the baby's name I made dinner as I did every evening since we had been living there. I moved slowly because I was in pain most of the time. This one night I was in too much pain and told my mother-in-law that I couldn't scrub the stove as I usually did nightly but I promised her I would do it first thing in the morning. Instead she told me no! I should rest and she would clean the stove. I told her not to do it. Because of her eyesight, my father-in-law did not allow her to do any work whatsoever; but she insisted, and I was too ill to say anymore. I fed my baby, put her to sleep, and said goodnight and went to bed. That night I was awakened out of a sound sleep by both my husband and father-in-law shaking me and cursing me for letting my mother-in-law clean the stove in her condition. The next morning while everyone was still sleeping I dressed my baby, went to the subway station and took the train home to my apartment, my own kitchen and living room. It is better to live in the corner of an attic than with a crabby woman in a lovely home (Proverbs 21:9). Later on my husband came home and was very apologetic over what had happened, and said it would never happen again.

As the days passed, I began feeling stronger and back to normal. I decided to take the baby to my mother's house. My father had not seen the baby yet, but when I got to the candy store, my father turned his back on me and refused to look at her. By now everybody knew the baby's name was, for the sake of the book "Ms. C" and I knew that that was a big part of his anger. I then went around the corner to visit my father's mother.

She also refused to call my baby by her name. It was she who also said that her son (my uncle) was to be chosen as the "best man" at my wedding, now said that he would be my baby's Godfather, and my husband's cousin who

34

she had chosen as my "maid of honor," would be the baby's Godmother. I then explained to her that…. I had no choice but to give them free reign over the wedding, but now I was a married woman with a husband as my partner, and we would be the ones deciding, on our own, what things affect our lives and to whom we connect our lives. When we decided to have the christening of the baby, we invited everyone from both of our families to our little apartment. Needless to say no one except my mother's sisters and brother came. My own mother was not allowed to come.

By the time my little girl was 5 months old we needed more room. We couldn't afford the rent for a larger apartment, therefore when we found a four-room apartment for $30 a month, we were overjoyed. The only stipulation for getting the apartment was that it was in a building that had 22 families, and was heated by coal. The apartment would only be rented to a family who would take the responsibility of Super and supplying the heat to the other 22 apartments. In order to do this we would have to go down into a huge basement where there was a gigantic furnace. Beside it was a pile of coal as big as the furnace itself. We would have to shovel that coal into the furnace at about 4:30 a.m. and every few hours thereafter. In late evenings we were to go down and "bank" the fire, which meant cleaning out the dead ashes and then get the fire to a certain level so that it would continue to burn throughout the night. It also meant that all the dead ashes had to be put in large trashcans and brought out for the garbage collection. We decided we would do this if it meant being able to afford an apartment. Philippians 4:13 say, *"I can do all things through Christ which strengtheneth me.*

We planned the schedule and moved in. the baby was now ready for a crib, which we couldn't afford. My mother's sister, Mildred, still had her baby's crib (from her baby Robert, we called him "Bobby") that was 20 years old, which she gave us. I will talk more about "Bobby," who had a special God-Ordained purpose in my life, later. The winter months came early, and for a short time, all was going well. Syl was still working nights at the airport, and when he came home, he would go into the basement and start up the furnace. During the day I would go down and check to make sure everything was working all right. I would leave the bady playing in the crib or sleeping and go down and check the fire. All was working out well until one morning I woke to find the apartment freezing cold and Syl was not there. Suddenly, there was a loud banging at the door; it was the tenants demanding to know why they had no heat. I ran down to the basement only to find him intoxicated on the pile of coal. I started up the furnace and ran back upstairs only to find my bady screaming, not knowing where I was. Yes, you guessed right, there was another apology and promise to change. And again, I not only forgave him, I believed him.

Unfortunately, instead of a change, matters just got worse; it occurred more and more. Not only could I not continue leaving my baby crying in the crib, I also could not promise the tenants that things would get better. I decided to tell the landlord that we would no longer take the responsibility of tending the furnace and that we would be out of the apartment before the next winter. In time we were told of another apartment one block away; we managed to save a little money in order to move. We did so and things started to calm down again. Once we were settled in, my mother-in-law asked us to come over because she had something to tell us. When we got there she said to us that since Syl was not earning enough money to adequately take care of his family that she was going to set him up in a business (beware of friendships bearing gifts). Believe not every spirit.... She was going to set him up as a partner in a bar with a family friend. Imagine a drunk running a bar; I couldn't believe what I was hearing. A bar! We returned home and I immediately called my mother-in-law to speak to her privately, expressing my concerns, since we both knew that Syl was a drinker. She said to me that that was his lot in life, so to speak. It was partially my fault, because he fell on my waxed floor and cut his arm, now she, as his mother would help him through his misfortune. Syl on the other hand was happy about it and I was naive enough to believe that his happiness would solve whatever was bothering him. The bar came through and Syl worked the day shift while his partner worked the night shift. Soon after the opening of the bar, I discovered that I was in my second pregnancy. Things got worse, about that time Syl's drinking had gotten out of control. He always managed to go to work, but never came home before 9 p.m. He usually staggered in about midnight. The only nights he came home on time was when he was too tired to stay out, at those times he came home and went to sleep. There was no conversation, we did nothing together, and we really had nothing in common to share with each other. I think if I had grown up in a normal household and had a normal childhood this would have bothered me, but since I was so used to being alone and not having anyone talk to me as a child, I just took it on the chin and hoped for the best. My hopes that he would stop drinking never faded.

My husband's drinking caused a great dilemma in my life and that affected me socially, economically, and mentally. I tried to resolve it the best way I could, but I see now that the methods I chose to resolve the problem were wrong. I did pray about the matter, but I now know that my approach in prayer was wrong. I had gone about it with the attitude that if he stopped drinking, it would make my life better. I now know that my real concern should have been for his soul and not the physical aspects of his demeanor; I wanted to build his self-esteem so that he would not have to depend on alcohol. If I had prayed for God to save his soul, my life with him would have been better and it would have brought with it self-esteem and no need for alcohol. I thought that self-esteem and having a son would give him the motivation not to drink. This didn't in any way diminish my love for our daughter. We loved her very much. Not knowing the Lord as I do now placed me in a dilemma. I was carnal in my thinking by focusing on the physical. Syl now had begun to drink so much that he had become known as the "Neighborhood and Town Drunk." People in the street would meet me and ask me why do I stay with him? God only knew the answer.

I remember sitting at home one night waiting for my husband to come, but as the night grew older I knew he wouldn't be coming home. The next day, although I was troubled, I decided not to stay in the house. I was now nine months pregnant with my second child and it was a beautiful day. I dressed the baby, put her in her stroller and went for a walk. As we passed the bar where he was half owner, I saw his car parked outside. Naturally, I went inside and found him sitting at the bar with another woman. I tapped him on the shoulder and told him that he should be home. The woman asked, "What do you want?" and I answered, "What do you want with my husband!" With that she spun around on the stool, lifting her leg as it swung into my stomach. There could have been a fight but the people there broke it up.

I went home, thinking he would come home also, but he didn't. He came home later that night and went directly to sleep. The next day, after work, he came home early with a bouquet of flowers and tears in his eyes. I remember my Bishop telling a story about a woman throwing all her boyfriend's clothes out of the window and the next day she was seen in the Laundromat washing those same clothes. That was only her boyfriend; this was my husband and perhaps my marriage.

Things were better between my mother-in-law and me. She had, by now, begun to call my bady by her name and soon after the birth of our son; I started to visit her more. Even my Father and his family were kinder when I brought the children over for them to see. When we planned the christening for my son, unlike it was with daughter's christening, this time they all acknowledged my son. It seemed that their past angers were gone, so I visited more often. I would bundle up my two babies and hop on the subway to visit my Mother-in-law in Jamaica. By this time, her eyesight was completely gone. So she never did get to see my son but she enjoyed holding and feeling his face. In the meantime, my husband's drinking worsened. I was not only concern with how often he got drunk, but now his drinking was turning into violent rages. When he was sober I would ask him if he had a grudge or situation that he would like to talk about. His answer was always no. He said that he really didn't know why he drank but one day he believed he would stop.

My mother-in-law knew of my husband's habitual drunkenness because there were many times at night when she called to speak with him and he wasn't home. She knew then to call him at the bar, only to learn from his partner that he was too sick to work and they had to come in to help. One day, out of the blue, my mother-in-law called and said that she knew that it wasn't easy for me. She went on to suggest that we move in with her. She said that she believed that my father-in-law would be a big help and she too would be able to help with the little things in spite of her sight. At this point I was willing to try anything in order to get some release and at the same time please my husband. I felt perhaps he would be happier nearer to his mother since the loss of her eyesight. Know this! I knew nothing about the favor of God and of the power of His blood, so I tried desperately to make sense of everything. God was in control of my life even then.

Praying always with all prayer and supplication in the Spirit, and watching thereunto with all perseverance and supplication for all saints;

Ephesians 6:18

By this time Mr. C had just turned two and her brother Mr. T was about three months. I talked it over with Syl and he agreed that we would move in. We moved into the basement apartment of my mother-in-law's house. A month later, my in-laws decided to visit their family in Austria and to leave us in charge of the house. All went well for a while, and then Syl's drinking became so violent that the neighbors had to get involved. Again and again, there was one apology after another. At this point his partner in the bar had had enough but offered to arrange for Syl to see a psychiatrist. When Syl was sober, he was always willing to do whatever it took to stop drinking. He did go; he even went as far as to have electric therapy. He stayed sober for a couple of weeks. When his parents returned from Italy, we decided not to tell them about the psychiatric therapy visits.

For we wrestle not against flesh and blood, but against principalities, against powers, against the rulers of the darkness of this world, against spiritual wickedness in high places.

Ephesians 6:12

One evening, after dinner Syl came home extremely intoxicated. My mother-in-law said nothing, but as I diapered the baby, she asked me if I would make her a cup of tea. I told her yes, as soon as I finished cleaning the baby. Syl, overheard my reply and immediately came over, pulled me by my hair, and dragged me over to the stove demanding that I make his mother the cup of tea immediately. I did so but later that night, I waited for Syl to fall asleep and then I called my brother. As I cried on the phone, I told him what had happen. My brother had witnessed, on numerous occasions, Syl's abusive behavior. Johnny, my brother was still living at home, so he couldn't bring me there. He knew my father would not take me in. My father had refused me once before, we still had a great fear of him. Instead Johnny told me to pack up the children and wait for him. He was there within 20 minutes. My in-laws were still awake when all this took place. I told them that I was leaving; they told me that I should not leave, but I thanked both of them for everything and left. That night my brother and I drove into Manhattan and found the least expensive hotel we could find. My brother paid for two nights in a room; in the meanwhile he looked around for an apartment for the children and me. He gave me a few dollars and told me he would be back the next day. The room only had one single bed, so I put my little girl to sleep first then laid my son next to her until he fell asleep. Fearing that my son would roll off the bed, I laid next to him but didn't sleep at all that night, fearful that I would rollover on him and suffocate him.

Early the next morning I realized I had nothing for them to eat. I locked the door and ran downstairs for some bread and a bottle of milk. Luckily there was a grocery store right next door. I filled the baby's bottle. he drank only milk and my little girl had milk and bread. I remembered trying to avoid the glaring and inquisitive eyes of the man at the desk as I passed. That day Johnny stopped by to tell me that he had found a two-room basement apartment that was very cheap. It was what I could afford, he took me to see it and I liked it. The landlady was very nice; I truthfully told her my situation. She was very compassionate and offered to help me with a few pieces of necessary furniture, including bedding, a kitchen table and chairs.

When I settled in, I called Joe at the bar (Syl's partner) to tell him I would need some living expenses and asked if he would arrange for me to receive money from Syl's pay for food and incidentals. I did not want Syl to not see the children but I felt it was best for us to separate. It was best for Joe to handle the money situation since he was put in charge of the arrangement at the bar by Syl's parents.

Joe did come by the first 2-3 weeks with money for us to live on. One day, he asked if Syl would be allowed to see the children at home. I agreed to the visits, but after the 3rd or 4th visit he told me that living with his parents was not right and that we should make a go of it alone. I agreed for the children's sake. I did not want a divorce.

It wasn't a month before Syl was back to drinking again. This time it seemed to lead to his deterioration and uncleanliness. Not just for days, but he went weeks at a time without taking a bath or shower. He developed a skin rash that spread not only on his face and neck but also over his entire body. He would scratch himself day and night to the point that blood oozed out of his body, face and neck. One night he came home from drinking while I had the children in the tub together. I asked him to get into the tub and play with them, because they hardly ever saw him. Most of the time they were asleep by the time he got home. I managed to persuade him to get into the tub; I told the children we were going to play a game with daddy to see who could scrub him the cleanest. That was the one time I was able to persuade him to take a bath. Weeks passed before he would bathe again.

The basement was getting tight. We looked for another apartment. This time we found a two-bedroom apartment behind a bakery. It was just a few blocks away from the candy store. One night my mom came over to see the children. Not realizing that Syl had been drinking, my mother who was sitting at the kitchen table witnessed Syl suddenly walk in with an angry attitude. He walked up to the table, picked it up and tossed it into the air. My mother was shook with fear. There was a married couple living upstairs who heard the commotion. The husband ran down the stairs and restrained Syl until he passed out. After calming my mother down, I told her to go home and not worry; everything would be all right. It brought back to my mind the time when he first put his hand through the window.

> *And fear not them which kill the body, but are not able to kill the soul: but rather fear*
> *him which is able to destroy both soul and body in hell.*
>
> *Matthews 10:28*

The drinking continued and now it was Joe who wanted out of the partnership. He called Syl's parents to tell them that he was releasing their son from their partnership agreement. As I said before the establishing of this business was the brainchild of Joe and Syl's parents. I had no say in the matter, neither did Syl. The agreement was made that Joe would be taking on a new partner, and Syl's obligation to the partnership was over and finished. Since he was not able to use his hand, Syl's parents already had another job for him. They arranged for him to drive a taxicab working nights. One day I took the children by subway to visit Syl's mother in Jamaica. During the visit I made a statement to her saying that I always put the children to bed early at about 6 p.m. and awaken them around 5 a.m. Her remark was, "why so early"? I explained to her that I trained them this way so that they would never see their father drunk.

My son, now was six and in kindergarten, and her brother was four and still at home. Once again Syl's drinking seemed to have lessened quite a bit. My father-in-law asked us if perhaps one day we would like to purchase a home. If so, and if I wanted to return to my sewing job he would be willing to keep my son at his house in Jamaica. We agreed, so Syl's father would meet me in the subway on Monday mornings to drop the baby off and again on Fridays for me to pick him up. For the next year or so, I almost never saw Syl because he worked nights and I worked days. The drinking actually did stop and the dream of buying a home was becoming reassuring.

About a year or so later we decided to take a ride to Long Island. The cheapest house we could afford required a $1,000.00 down payment, which we did not completely have. We asked both our parents for a loan but they said this is something we would have to do on our own. I continued to work for another year to save the thousand dollars we needed for the down payment. We did manage to purchase a small house and move in.

Once we were in the house I thanked my father-in-law for taking care of the baby all those weeks. I told him also that we would be keeping him home with us from then on. He agreed that a child should be home with his parents, though I knew he was somewhat sad because he and my son had developed a bond with each other. My father-in-law was truly a good-hearted man. We were able to pay expenses of living in a new house in Long Island with the exception of cost of doing things around the house such as plumbing, electrical, roofing, etc. There was also the mowing of the lawn and the shoveling of the snow. Syl could not tackle any of these jobs because of his hand. I would do all the mowing and the shoveling. I didn't mind, I was so happy to have a home and peace and quiet. Syl was yet out of his habit of drinking, but what I was starting to notice was his disinterest of anything related to the up keep of a home. We never really sat at the table together for dinner as a family mainly because he worked nights. I felt so close with my children, it seemed that the whole world revolved around just them and me. It was starting to think that I was husband and wife plus mother and father.

Maintenance of the house was starting to increase to a point that it affected our ability to pay our bills. It was now time for my little boy to start school; this forced me to look for a job in my field of work. There was a sweater factory not too far away that was hiring seamstresses. I discussed it with Syl and he was very agreeable with me going back to work. All I had to do was send the children off to school in the morning while Syl slept. I would be home in the afternoon when they came home and Syl would leave for work again. He worked six days a week including Saturday and Sunday; so we were really never together.

With my first one or two paychecks I decided to buy an outdoor gym set for the children. It was delivered to our house unassembled. I thought that Syl would be able to help, just a little, with putting it together, and that it would create a little interest and excitement for him. But as it turned out he would always be getting up just in time to have breakfast and leave for work. So on Saturday I followed all the instructions and in a matter of hours the gym was ready. What followed after putting it together was really very funny. I put the children on the swings and as they were swinging, I saw that the swing was about to topple over. I stopped immediately and thought about what was happening. There were four metal legs that held up the swing, and they would rise up off the ground whenever the children swung high. The children and I went to the hardware store and I bought a bag of cement and poured it into a big tub. I dug four holes under where the metal legs were standing. We then mixed the cement with water and poured it into the four holes. Then we balanced the four legs into the holes. We then waited a day or two until the cement hardened. It seemed that the job was accomplished and my children were a part of solving the problem. I thank God for the relationship between my children and me.

For almost two years there were many instances when the bonding between my children and me was inseparable. One day my next-door neighbor came out and admired the gym and swing set. She told me how she watched me and the children put it together and then added, "And your husband didn't help you one bit." Those biting words did something to me that sunk very deeply in my spirit. Even today, after almost fifty years, I can still hear those words loud and clear.

At that time I did not know the Lord, I simply knew of Him. Therefore, when He spoke to me I could not hear Him, since only his sheep hears his voice. I did not answer her, but I could feel anger and resentment welling up inside me. Not at her, but I had come to the realization that I no longer wanted to be the man of the house. Soon after that, my job closed and I had to start looking for work, but the only other sweater factories in business were in the city. I came across a newspaper ad advertising a daytime shift for a female bartender, no experience necessary. I told Syl about it and he had no problem with it. Actually Syl really never objected to anything since he lived in his own world. Even the disciplining of the children he would never share in.

I went to see about the job and was hired. I learned very quickly and needless to say in comparison to the sweater factory, I learned of a different life style and developed a different social life. I was also becoming aware of an independence that I never experienced before, but keep in mind, "the devil comes to steal, kill and destroy."

After a couple of months I met man, we'll call him Mr. J, who came in for a nightcap after work, just as I was getting off duty. We talked a few minutes and I told him I had to leave to go home to my children. The next day he came in again, except this time he came in a few hours earlier. He sat at the bar and talked to me when I was not waiting on customers. This went on and eventually he asked me to have a cup of coffee with him after work. I told him no I had to get home. He then asked if he could see me for the cup of coffee on my day off during the week.

In whom the god of this world hath blinded the minds of them which believe not, lest the light of the glorious gospel of Christ, who is the image of God, should shine unto them.

2 Corinthians 4:4

The children were in school and Syl would be sleeping or watching television. I found myself drawn to him or drawn to the fact that he found me interesting, I don't know which. I do know that I no longer felt like a man. We met often after that and he went on to tell me he was separated from his wife and he also had two small children. I fell deeply in love with him and before I knew it I was telling Syl that I could not go on with our marriage. He did not want to break up the marriage but I was convinced that to him our marriage had turned into a comfort zone. I was not hearing from him a good reason for continuing our marriage, and that's what I wanted to hear.

We did divorce and the house was sold for exactly the amount it was purchased for. I did not feel guilty leaving Syl, and as far as my children were concerned, I thought the divorce would give me a chance to give them a more rounded family life. I was in the world and outside of the ark of safety. How can you think straight without the Holy Ghost? If I had met Jesus like the man at the pool, I am sure he would have supplied me with the wisdom I was lacking.

The children and I moved back to Queens, NY and settled into a one-bedroom apartment not too far from my father's candy store. The children settled into a local school and I went to work in a sweater factory close by. If there was confusion in their hearts, I was either too selfish to see it or I was in denial that I had not put them first. I kept telling myself that they were being shorted of a complete family. All I remember is sitting them down and telling them that their father and I were divorced and that they would be seeing him every other Saturday and that I never wanted to hear them say anything against him and if they did, they would be punished severely by me. It was very important to me that they should always respect him and that in due time they would come to understand.

In the meantime, Mr. J also divorced and we continued seeing each other. I also continued working in the sweater factor; the manager took a special liking to me and we became very close friends. Her name was Virginia and she invited the children, Mr J and me to her home along with her husband for dinner. We told her we were planning to marry and they were delighted. We became such good friends that we asked them if they would stand up with us at our wedding. They agreed and we were married six months later.

The one bedroom apartment was now inconvenient and children were now ten and twelve years old. We moved again into a three-bedroom apartment. We moved so many times during those years that I realized that the moving and changing schools constantly were forms of abuse in raising my children. After two months of being married, Mr. J decided he could not find a steady job and that he would be better off taking on odd jobs as long as I was able to work and pay the bills; he convinced me that it would be easier on me if he stayed at home doing chores around the house while I worked and the children were in school. After I got home from work we would have dinner together. I kept telling myself that this was what I wanted all along, a family togetherness.

Soon after I discovered I was pregnant, Mr. J was happy at first, but still was not working except for one or two days per week and that didn't go too far after he would send support to his own children. We knew things were not going well, so we decided to give up the apartment and look for something cheaper. We found a cold flat apartment near the candy store that had no flooring and broken down walls but Mr. J said he would work on it when he wasn't working. In the meantime, off went the children again to a different school. I think they were comfortable because they could walk over to grandma's store after school. They were very obedient children and never said a word of disrespect to me or anyone else. But Mr. J never did find a job and never fixed the apartment. Instead he started seeing other women. We had a confrontation and he admitted he never should have married since he was not the type to be "tied down" to any women, much less have to go to work every day. He just wanted a carefree lifestyle.

That night I had a miscarriage at two months. He left the next day and I never saw him again. My friend Virginia was devastated over the breakup and continued to visit us and invite us over. I continued to work with her and managed to pay the rent and support the children along with a little child support money from Syl.

Syl had mentioned at one time of us getting back together, but I just did not want to. As I said before by this time I was convinced more than ever that my children and I were extraordinarily close and tightly knitted and that we could go through anything together. My father in the meantime was still very cold to me although he was more pleasant to the children than he ever was.

> Be kind and compassionate to one another, forgiving each other, just as in Christ God forgave you.
>
> Ephesians 4:32

One day Virginia paid a visit to my father's store. She never went in full detail of what she said to him, but suddenly his attitude towards me changed and he became more kind. I would go to the candy store with the children on Saturdays when there was no work or school. He would give the children anything they wanted; ice cream, soda, candy and etc. When there were no customers we would sit and talk. The past was never mentioned or brought up. I was just so happy he was talking to me; nothing else mattered. Shortly after that my father got very sick; his leg developed ulcers due to diabetes and he was bed ridden. Their apartment was right above the candy store but he was not even able to get out of bed. My mother had to open the store at 6 a.m. and stay until 11 p.m. My brothers were already married and responsible for their own families, so they helped as much as possible. My father was taken by ambulance because gangrene settled in his leg. I quit my job to work full time in the candy store, explaining to Virginia the problem. She completely agreed and of course we remained friends.

My father was in the hospital for a full three months and every night one of us would stay in the candy store and the rest would be at the hospital. One day we were told that he would have his leg removed because the gangrene had spread out of control. I remember going in the room alone and embracing him, crying out, "no, don't let them do that." He looked at me and cried, "Alright if you don't want me to I won't." But the doctors all spoke to my mother and brother and convinced us all that it had to be done. He did have the amputation and we spent the next two weeks with him in the hospital. One night I decided to go to the hospital before anyone else was due up there. I walked in the room and the nurse told me he was developing a high fever. I remember saying the Lord's Prayer and the Hail Mary. I knew God heard me because that's all I knew. Suddenly my father turned to me and said looking over to the corner of the room, "Look at that fire over there." I turned to see but there was no fire. As I turned back to him, he closed his eyes and passed away.

I don't know if it was the high fever that caused my father to think he saw fire but the bible tells me that fire is the presence of the Holy Ghost and I prefer to believe the latter. I may not have had a Bible then but I believed with all my heart that my father repented. Now of course I knew my mother would be alone so I talked to Virginia and told her I would be leaving the job to work steadily in the candy store. She assured me I was doing the right thing. My mother and I started to cook breakfast and lunches in the store, which enabled us to close nightly at 8 p.m. instead of 11. My father had left a small amount of money and my mother gave a little to my two brothers and me to share. With this I was able to buy a used car and get a nicer apartment and once again move the children to a different school. I was able to drive to the store to relieve my mother and the children would go home with her and do their homework until I came in. I told the children that this move was for the better, and they would have their own bedrooms. We did live there for one year, after which my mother's landlord told her she had to move or pay triple the rent. She knew she could not do this. I asked her if she still had anything left from my father's money. She told me she only had a few thousand dollars. I had no money at all, but I suggested we look for a small house that would only require half of the money she had, and I would pay the mortgage as my half. She agreed and we took a ride to Glendale and found a small two family house.

The house consisted of three rooms on the first floor and three rooms on the second floor. The price was exactly double of what my mother had so we purchased the house and I took over the mortgage and all the bills, including the taxes. I asked my mother to pay only seventy-five dollars a month to help me out. She was delighted with the way things worked out. The children were happy about the move because the house was near a school they had already been in a few years ago.

In the meantime, I still worked in the candy store. The same landlord who owned the apartment above the store told us he had no choice but to raise the rent on the store. Business at that time was down to nothing so we decided to close the store for good. The house we bought was actually in the heart of the sweater industry. I did not go back to work with Virginia because that factory had closed, but I did find another job in the same area. By this time my children were eleven and thirteen and it seemed we were finally getting our lives on track. But before we actually closed the candy store I became good friends with one of the local customers. Actually he was a neighbor who lived near the store and we knew each other for many years. He had known Syl and the kind of life I had lived with him, he also knew of the marriage to Mr. J although he never knew him directly.

He was a good friend of the family for years. We used to talk in the store a lot and I felt an attraction towards him. We dated a few times and then I told him we would be closing the store and moving. He was very kind and loving, especially towards my mother and that meant a lot to me. He said he would call and visit after we were settled. He did just that; my children liked him very much. We continued to date and he sometime came over just to watch TV with us. His name is not important but he was called by his nickname "Buby." I saw in him the strength I always wanted in a man but never could find. I found myself comparing his strength to that of my father's, with the exception that my father's strength was dominated by meanness and abusiveness. Buby's strengths were kindness and sincerity.

We continued dating and eventually I started noticing there was never any mention of commitment. I felt we were not children, and had no qualms in bringing up the subject. In as nice a way as possible he made me know

49

he would never marry. He was never married before and had no children, but he had a mother, 3 sisters, nieces and nephews all whom he loved very much and they in turn treated him as a king and he enjoyed every minute of it. He was so truthful and sincere. I knew he wasn't a liar because I had also known his entire family; somehow, I felt in time he would have a change of heart. My children did not mind us not marrying they had a closeness with him whenever they saw him that was warm and gentle. They also could see that for the first time I was happy, so our relationship continued.

After about seven years in the relationship, I found myself pregnant. I never told my children although I sensed that my mother knew. I wasn't sure of the kind of response I was going to get from him, but somehow I knew I wouldn't get the answer I was hoping for. When I told him, he was unsurprisingly quiet for a while, and then added, "We'll work it out." The next day he told me of a doctor whom we all knew. Almost everybody in the neighborhood was a patient. In fact I had even taken my own children to him when they were small for their vaccinations. I knew that Buby had a tremendous fear of having to make a commitment and taking the responsibility for rearing a family. I wanted this baby desperately. I realized how intent he was on not being a father; therefore, I started to consider having the baby regardless of the circumstances. However the thought of my children disgraced in the neighborhood made me have a change of heart. I just couldn't let them go through that. And so I found myself in the doctor's office going through what I had been convinced as the right thing to do. After the ordeal, I continued to work and said nothing to the children. I saw Buby a few times after that and I could see in his eyes that he was sorry; but by now feeling nothing good would ever come of it, I was determined to end the relationship. Like the man at the pool, I had a condition that no one could help me with and once again I was doing it my way. Unknowingly, God was still in control, directing my path.

The next few years were spent solely with my children, my mother, and work. My daughter now seventeen and my son fifteen were now able to care for themselves. One day I bought tickets to take my mom to see a Broadway play. We drove into the city to see the play and got out about

11pm. On our way home, we drove over the 59th street Bridge onto Queens Blvd, in Long Island City. We both were hungry and we decided to stop at a Chinese Restaurant. It was late and they were about to close since there were no other customers. They let us in and we sat towards the back. As we were dining I saw a man come in and go to the register. I then noticed the manger hand him money from the cash box. I stood up in the aisle sensing something wrong. The man saw me and immediately took a gun and fired it. He then ran out to a waiting car and left. The owner had by this time called the police and when they arrived, they found a bullet in the wall exactly about an inch from where I was standing. As frightened as we were I thanked God that we were not killed.

> *Are they not all ministering spirits, sent forth to minister for them who shall be heirs of salvation?*
>
> *Hebrews 1:14*

I noticed that I was now becoming more interested in Tarot Cards, Fortune Telling, Tea Leaves, Crystal Balls, and Ouija boards. I was now delving more and more into the occult. I found myself more and more visiting Psychics, Tarot Card Readers, and Fortune Tellers. I even invited them into my home. After being introduced to the Ouija Board, I found all too soon that it was not a game. My grandmother was into the occult and had taught me all that I knew about the subject, but what I was now discovering was much greater than anything she told me. I now was going to séances, even hosting them in my home; worse than that I had my daughter invite her friend from next door. I remember while during the séance ritual the table we were sitting at rose a few inches off the floor; we all became so frightened we stopped immediately. We agreed we would never do a séance again, but I could not give up the rest of the occult. Sometimes we don't hear the voice of God as the Holy Spirit speaks. Paul said in Hebrews, "Oh, that today you would listen as he speaks," (Hebrews 3:7).

Earlier I mentioned my cousin Bobby whom I loved very much, the one thing we had in common was our involvement in the occult. Every time I spoke with him he had found something new. Among other things was his discovery of numerology and how he ran his life by it. This went on for a number of years but one day while visiting at my aunt's house, my cousin Bobby shared with me what a joyful and awesome experience he had serving Jesus. He told me how serving Jesus had turned his life around, that I could have this same experience, just for the asking.

It seemed that whatever Bobby and I talked about always lead back to Jesus. I loved Bobby very much from our childhood, but I could not get out of my mind that this was the same cousin who as a teenager in the park with a friend, robbed an elderly man sitting on a bench; they beat him so badly that he died. Who my uncle knew, I do not know, but my cousin never spent a day in prison. I just never could understand how someone who did so many bad things could talk about Jesus. I know now that Jesus can change anybody's life; after all the Bible says, a prophet is not honored in his own country and one's family can be considered a country. If anyone can talk about Jesus, surely it would be Bobby and me; after all look at Paul, God changed him from persecutor to preacher.

> *For all have sinned and come short of the Glory of God*
>
> *Romans 3:23*

At that time I told him that I was happy for him, but following Jesus was not for me. I just went about my normal daily routine. I had not gone out much socially, so I decided to go to a local neighborhood dance. At this dance I met Joe.

Joe had leadership qualities that I greatly admired. We had dated only a couple of times before I discovered that he was a member of the Mafia. Since I had often seen them in my father's candy store, I was not a stranger to the Mafia family. Therefore, the fact that Joe was a member didn't bother me. All I knew of them was that they were perfect gentlemen. After dating Joe for three months, one night while he was taking me home, he said to me "before I take you home I have to first meet a friend who is to deliver something to me." I was to take the ride with him, and after we met the friend, he would take me home. But that particular evening I was not feeling well so I asked him to take me home first. He did so and went back to the "club" where he was to meet his friend. The next morning as I watched the morning news, there was a shooting in a "club" and two people were shot and killed execution style. One of them was Joe and all

I could do was lament sorrowfully. I didn't know then that God was in control of my life. I was waiting like the man at the pool. My cousin had tried to help me get to the troubling water but I was too busy doing it my own way.

But God shows His love for us in that while we were still sinners, Christ died for us
Romans 5:8

My cousin Bobby who was now married and living in Wheeling, West Virginia came to mind. I called him to tell him that I would be coming to visit for a few days. I did and after arriving at Bobby's house, we spent the next few days just sharing. One day we got around to talking about Joe. I asked Bobby why did Joe have to die such a violent death; his response was "who died more violently than Christ?" When it was time for me to leave he gave me a Bible and told me that I could read it whenever I felt I wanted to. It reminded me of when my grandmother gave me her recipe and told me I did not have to use it until I was ready.

When I got back to New York, I put the Bible on the shelf, feeling that God and religion was for Bobby and not for me. I personally thought religion was another way for Bobby to express his beliefs in the occult, or resolve himself of the guilt of the incident in the park with the old man on the park bench. In the meantime, I was still looking for answers through the occult. I went to see a fortune-teller to whom I mentioned Joe by name. I asked her nothing other than if Joe loved me. I was now starting to question the validity of Astrology and the occult. I was shocked when she said, "He is no longer with you." Believing the fortune teller seemed so right because all around her were religious statues of various saints, lighted candles, and even a crucifix on the wall with Jesus hanging on it. The room was also filled with the fragrance of incense. I felt more, as if I were in church. The crucifix did nothing for me; it did not touch me in a personal way. Later on in this book you will see how Jesus personally spoke to me concerning the cross.

For false Christs and false prophets will arise and perform great signs and wonders, so as to lead astray, if possible, even the elect.
Matthews 2:24

As time moved on, I spent the next four years of my life living as usual. By now the children were about 20 years old and as with children that age we were starting to fuss and argue a lot, mainly because I thought we would forever be right. Actually we were but I had not accepted the fact that we were not solely a threesome anymore. As a result, I became more strict, over-bearing and domineering. For a year or so there was a break in our relationship, which lead to me telling them to leave the house if they could not abide by the rules. Later I became very distraught about my decision that one evening while my son sat on a neighbor's stoop with some of his friends, I went outside and embarrassed him in such a way I cannot ever put in a book. I went back in the house and looked at the many pictures I had of the children displayed on the wall. I took them down and destroyed every one of them. As they say, "a rat can get in the house through a crack in the door, but once he's in, he's in," and my house was full of them. The relationship between my children and me was at an all-time low.

There came a time when I was asked by a friend to go out for a drink. She and I went to a local bar and began to socialize with some of the other bar goers. And there I met a man who would eventually become my third husband, let's call him Mr. V. As I sit here and write, my spirit brings back to memory two things. I remember as clear as day when my father brought home that package of writing paper and how delighted I was. I see now God's hand in the entire ordeal. Secondly, I had tried writing this story many times but I always had a hard time focusing, so one day I decided to do my writing in my local library. I thought that I could concentrate better there. From the first day I went the writing began. It amazes me how God moved in his plan for my life. I had spent much of my childhood in the solitude of the local library; it was the one place where I felt at peace whenever I could get away. Now I find myself at the local library once again as a part of God's predestined will writing how the move of God has become evident of his purpose for me. I know He has preserved me all these years for such a time as this and has had His angels around me all the time. He has never left or forsaken me in spite of the fact that I neither knew Him nor His promises for me through the Word of God, yet He continued to wait for me as I lay at the pool. More and more I found myself looking back regretting not having the traditional all American family with a husband, wife and two children. I found myself regretting those years of unfulfilled joy. I always knew assuredly that there was more out there for me.

> *For in the day of trouble He will conceal me in His tabernacle, in the secret place of His tent He will hide me, He will lift me up on a rock.*
>
> *Psalm 27:7*

After meeting Mr. V in the local bar, we started talking regularly. He seemed very polite therefore I wasn't hesitant to accept his invitation to see him again. We continued to see each other for a while. I eventually introduced him to my children and my mother. Everyone got along quite well with him, and after about six months he asked me to marry him. I was now sure that my life was finally making a turn for the better. There was no reason for me to turn to organized religion as Bobby had done. I didn't know that I was still at the pool waiting for Jesus to stop by. I felt that Mr. V was the answer to my problem and there was surely no need to go searching for anything else. After all, why look for Jesus when things are going well, right?

> *In all your ways acknowledge Him and He will make straight your paths*
>
> *Proverbs 3:6*

Thinking back, I see now, with the Holy Ghost (which came to guide and teach me) that I could have received the message that the Lord was giving me earlier in my relationship with Him. Let me explain – One day, before Mr. V and I were married, we took a trip to upstate New York. As we walked around the town, I noticed a church that I felt a strong desire to just go in and visit. No matter how much I begged and tried to convince Mr. V to let me go in for a few minutes, if just to look inside, he absolutely refused, and became angry. I didn't know it then but I know now that there were powerful satanic forces at work trying to prevent me from hearing and obeying the voice of God.

I hadn't been in close contact with my friend Virginia for some years because I was always working, and she lived in Elmont, LI. I called her to tell her of my upcoming marriage and she invited us to visit. We went and had a nice time; Virginia seemed to like Mr. V. Also, I know she was happy for me. As we planned the marriage there was one thing I still hungered for and that was to raise children again but this time with a husband at my side.

My own children were already grown. Although my daughter was working, she rented the basement apartment and my son was now married and lived a few blocks away. I was convinced that I could relive my life, correct the past, and regain the stolen years of yesterday. Mr. V in the meantime moved in with me and we set a date to marry within six months. He worked nights, while I still worked days in the sweater factory. Even though my children and I did not speak of the past, I felt we had lost a lot of closeness. I suppose that is why I didn't believe my daughter when she came home one night high on drugs and screamed out how Mr. V would come home from work late at night and tap on her basement window to get her attention and ask her if she needed some company. I told myself she said these things because she was angry with me because of the arguments we had had in the past. I thought that those ugly issues would not rear their heads in my life again. I told Mr. V about it and he convinced me that she was mistaken. It was never mentioned again.

> *But solid food is for the mature, for those who have their powers of discernment trained by constant practice to distinguish good from evil*
>
> *Hebrews 5:14*

In the meantime, I was determined to have children to raise with a husband. Not being able to have children anymore, I looked into fostering. As if that wasn't enough, I still had a burning desire to go back to Long Island to live. After we were married, we decided to sell the house and use the money to buy another house on Long Island. Years passed and by now the price of houses had gone up drastically. The cheapest house we could afford was seventy miles away. Mr. V was in total agreement with the move and the plan to become foster parents. When I told my mother, she was very upset with the move. She hated the idea of going so far away. I explained to her that she could not financially afford to stay in the city on her own. Knowing this she reluctantly came with us. When we moved I applied for the foster children and soon I had a house full. I had children of all faiths. Although I was not yet saved, I loved to take the children to different churches for Sunday services. Knowing nothing except Catholicism all my life, I found it interesting to share in Communion in a Methodist Church. We always said grace at the table and talked about God. For some reason, I felt moved to share this with them, knowing they were lost and confused. I suppose I did not feel this way about my own children since I thought we were so tight. I see now that training your children in the way they should go includes training yourself first. Paul said to the Church of Roman that, *"by the deeds of the law there shall no flesh be justified in His sight,"* (Romans 3:20). You can't just say grace because it's the rule of the family. In the meantime, Mr. V was driving to the city every day to work and it was taking a toll on him. I had a little money left over from the sale of my house in Queens, so we found a small hardware store on Long Island very cheap. We brought the store and Mr. V worked in it while I took care of the children. It also gave me a chance to be with my mother, since she had no way of getting around without knowing how to drive.

The hardware store had to be open daily and Mr.V had no days off to rest. I told him I could open the store and work there two day a week, so that he could be home. All he had to do was to supervise the children when they came home from school. He was very happy about the situation. Things were working out pretty well for a while. I started noticing my mother becoming very distant from Mr. V and on the days he was home she would stay in her room and not come out. I told myself she was still angry with us for moving out there. I also started noticing, the children becoming distant when eh would walk into the room, in spite of becoming very close to me, even to the point where they called me "mom." I also dismissed this as he was extremely stern and strict with the boys, (not with the girls). I had mentioned this to the Social Worker when she visited me but she assured me that the children needed to be disciplined and not to be babied or treated special.

> *Oh foolish Galatians, who hath bewitched you, that ye should not obey the truth,*
> *before whose eyes Jesus Christ hath been evidently set forth, crucified among you.*
> *Galatians 3:1*

A few months later I received a telephone call from my Social Workers asking if she could come to the house while the children were in school. I was not prepared for the bombshell that I got that day. I was told that my twelve-year-old foster daughter told her that Mr. V attempted to sexually molest her. After I came to my senses somewhat, I told her I did not believe it and was told by other foster mothers, that sometimes children would say things like that in hopes that they would be sent back to their own biological parents. She then told me that before she spoke to me, she had a meeting with my sixteen-year-old foster daughter, and she too had to avoid him. She then showed me a necklace that he gave her; telling her that it was a secret between him and her. She never told me because she did not want to hurt me but she did tell daughter, that explained why she was so moved by it that she thought she would protect Robin (the sixteen year old) but she did not realize Mr. V was molesting the twelve year old also. The Social Worker said she had no choice but to remove all the children from the home. That was a day that will live with me all my life. That night I waited for him to come home. He was surprised to see the children not there. I confronted him and told him to leave. He did so.

I had no choice but to open the store the next day. Whatever was going on in my mind I had to put it on hold. Whatever was going on in my heart would have to wait. Not so much because of the store, but mainly because I couldn't handle it. That morning when I opened the store, I found Mr.V sitting in a chair with a bottle of scotch next to him almost empty. All my hopes of this being a bad dream just blew up in my face. He left the store and I did not see him again. I worked in the store every day after that. About two weeks later a detective assigned to the case came in to talk to me. He assured me that I was cleared of any charges but they were trying to locate Mr. V He kept in contact with me and a few weeks later he called to tell me that Mr. V was in police custody. He said he would keep me informed and up to date. The end result was that Mr.V served a six-month prison sentence and got five years of probation. In the meantime not only could I not bear the emptiness of losing and missing the children, but also my mother was alone in the house everyday with nowhere to go because I was confined to the store. I don't know what broke my heart more the children all gone or my mother wasting away in what was to her a barren land. I had to resolve both issues; I felt that selling the house would not only alleviate memories, but would also resolve the problem of my mom's loneliness.

The Lord shall preserve thee from all evil, He shall preserve thy soul.
Psalm 121:7

I still didn't want to come back to the city, so again I looked for a small house not only closer to the hardware store, but also along a main street where my mother could go walking and shopping whenever she wanted to. I found it and settled my mom in, confident that she would be more content there. Once again moving was not the answer; reality started to set in and I began agonizing over the loss of my foster children. I had learned to love them individually so much. I know they loved me, which made it so hard for them to try to keep Mr.V's molesting them from me. All the while my daughter was trying to protect the girls and spare me the pain.

I called Virginia one day from the store and blurted out to her what happened. She immediately came over and we talked. Virginia was a very calm, quiet, reserved woman and just allowed me to vent. She spoke of peace to me and told me there is a reason for everything and in time I will be able to understand it all. I loved her for her sincere friendship, but could see no logic in what she said. That was the first time I desperately looked for an answer through religion, not knowing I was at the pool waiting for Jesus to come. I cried to God that night alone in my bedroom. As I was going over my life, I let out a deafening scream, asking him WHY??? I received no response. How can you hear a response when you do not know who it is that you are talking to? A few weeks later my nephew had graduated from school and they were having a party in Queens. My mom and I drove to Queens that night. I wasn't really looking forward to seeing everyone and facing all the pitiful looks.

A NEW CREATURE

I reluctantly stayed at the party, not really communicating much with anyone; relatives would come over and touch my shoulder and ask me sadly, "How are you doing RoRo?" I would just tell them I am doing well and go on to another subject. Heaviness came over me and I decided I would have a glass of wine. Before I knew it, I had 4-5 glasses of wine. It was now about 11pm. I suddenly got myself up and went over to the phone booth and called Virginia. I didn't ask her, I told her I was coming over to her house. She asked if I was drinking and I told her yes and hung up. With that, I knew mom would enjoy a few days in Queens at my brother's house so I asked her and she was delighted to go. They told me I was in no condition to drive, but I turned and left. I had a vague idea of where Virginia's house was, so I got on the highway going against the traffic. I was able to immediately get off of the exit and find the right entrance. It was 1 a.m. by the time I found her house. When she opened the door she found a babbling drunken fool. And all she said was "Come in Rose." I didn't even have the sense to apologize for the late hour. She had coffee for me and we sat at her kitchen table for at least 2 hours. She waited till I was cried out and there were no more tears left. Then she mentioned in a peaceful and loving voice, JESUS.

No one can come to me unless the Father who Sent me draws him, and I will raise him up on the last day

John 6:44

For it is written, He will command His angels concerning you to guard you carefully.
Luke 4:10

She spoke for a long while and I sat in complete astonishment, hearing things that I had never heard before. Looking back, I know that I was "the man at the pool" waiting for Jesus to make an appearance; only this time I would recognize him. After a couple of hours she gave me a nightgown to sleep in, but before I slept, she prayed with me.

THEN CAME THE MORNING.......

The next day I awoke and mentioned to Virginia how refreshed I was after the most peaceful night of sleep in a long time. She smiled and then went on to suggest that when I went home I should look for a Pentecostal church in my area, since I lived about fifty miles past her on Long Island. She prayed again with me after which I thanked her for all she had done and went home.

The next evening when I got home from work I asked God to show me a Pentecostal church, since I had never even heard the word before. I looked in the telephone directory and standing out, as though it was jumping off the page was a church about ten blocks from my house. I called and received a message giving the church schedule. I went there the next night only to meet the Pastor and his wife in the office. There was no service that night but they were there in the office. They invited me in and I introduced myself to them. They were very loving and asked if they could be of some help. It was then that I once again broke down and blurted out the agonizing experience of my husband's molesting the children. They invited me to their church service on that coming Wednesday night. I mentioned the fact that I was raised as a Catholic and to my surprise, I was told that both the Pastor and his wife were also raised Catholic. He then reached over and handed me a tape. I noticed the date on the tape was dated the exact previous Sunday. He said it was his sermon he just preached a few days earlier.

I thanked him, but explained that I did not have a tape player. He then went to the other room and brought out a tape player for me to take home. Living in a world of distrust of anything or anyone, I turned to him and said in an indignant tone of voice, "I don't know you and you don't know me and for all you know I may never come back to return the tape." The answer he gave me shocked me and left me dumbfounded. He simply said, "Well, I don't know you and you don't know me, and if I never see you again, it's okay" I was left so speechless; I barely got the words, "thank you" out.

I had to go to work the next day so I decided to take the tape and player to my job and listen to it in my free time. After I heard the tape I double-checked the date that was on it. Sure enough, there was no mistake. This sermon was given just the Sunday prior to my meeting the Pastor. The sermon was an illustration of my entire life. The title on the front of the tape was "Philippians 3:13." My anger, bitterness, hard-heartedness and distrust left me and through my tears I saw clearly myself waiting at the pool and that this tape (the pastor and his wife) was a type of Christ meeting me at the pool.

And he believed the Lord and He counted it to him as righteousness
Genesis 15:6

I had a burning desire to go to the church, but since I had to work on Sunday's I went to see what other times they were there. There was a fellowship there on Wednesday evenings. I decided to go and also bring back the tape player. But Satan was going to try to prevent me from going there. As I was driving I started having feelings of doubt and guilt. But the guilt was of going to another church other than where I was raised, the Catholic Church. I started to doubt whether God would approve of me going to a different church, even though in my heart I never doubted him.

In just those few days I learned one thing from God. He loved me and would answer me. So I had a little talk with him and asked him if I should visit this church. The moment I asked him, I looked up at the sky and I saw a gigantic cloud in the formation of a cross. I had never seen it before and I never saw it again. When I walked into the church that night there was singing and music. It was a relatively quiet evening. The pastor was speaking but I knew absolutely nothing of the order of the service. I saw and heard nothing that I can say I ever saw or heard before. Suddenly the Pastor motioned to me to come to the altar. That was something I had never seen done in a Catholic church and I had not the slightest idea of what to do when I got up there. All I know is that I was there with a heavy heart. Some of the folks there started to gather around and suddenly the pastor bent down from the altar and laid his hand on my head. This was also something I had never seen before nor had any idea of the purpose of it. All I do remember is that the minute his hand touched me I found myself being picked up from the floor; I have never been the same.

> *And He stretched out His hand and touched him, saying, I am willing, be cleansed,*
> *and immediately the leprosy left him.*
>
> *Luke 5:13*

Later, a woman came to me and said, "You have a sweet spirit," but I had no idea why she said it. My cousin Bobby whom I have mentioned earlier had passed away a couple of years earlier. I still had the Bible he gave me nine years ago even though I never read it. I had it tucked away. I went home that night and got it out and read it from Genesis to Revelation. It wasn't that I found a church, but that I found God, the true and living God...not through an idolatrous, religion, rituals or even the occult. Perhaps, I was searching all this time through man-made relationships for God. I now realized that although I never knew him, He loved me. The one thing I now know is I want to forget the past, and go on with Jesus.

In the meantime, my daughter was going through trials and tribulation of her own; I told her of the love of Jesus and what he did for me. She came to the church one night, found Jesus and never has turned back. I also brought my mother one night and she was in awe; she also has no desire to return to the Catholic Church. I found that I had a hunger for God that grew stronger and stronger, wanting to be in church more than just on Wednesday nights. I prayed for God to free me of Sunday work and he did in his own time.

> *And they said, Believe on the Lord Jesus Christ, and thou shalt be saved, you and*
> *your household.*
>
> *Acts 16:31*

One day I was reading the Word and God spoke to me and told me my body was the temple of God. I had become a chain smoker at two packs a day. The Holy Spirit was tugging at me and telling me this was not his will. Being a babe in Christ I was not sure if this was Him. I asked God for a sign if he wanted me to quit smoking. The moment I asked, my entire tongue blew up the size of a balloon. It stayed blown up for two days. Trying to convince myself it was a coincidence, I started to smoke again. Again after the first cigarette, my tongue blew up. This time I knew it was the Lord, but I realized I could not give up smoking. I prayed the Lord would make a way. The next day I was home and the phone rang. When I answered, it was a little girl who I later learned had dialed the wrong number. She thought she was talking to her aunt. She was begging on the phone for her aunt to come and get her away from her stepfather who was always touching her body. Before I could get any information as to her whereabouts she hung up saying he was at the door. I called the operator to trace the call but she couldn't. I called the police and there was not enough for them to do anything. As I cringed under the pressure I went in my secret prayer closet and cried out to the Lord.

"Lord, no matter what it takes, save this child, and I promise, a solemn oath, I will never smoke a cigarette again." As soon as I said it, I began to regret and ask forgiveness because I knew I was about to break my vow in about twenty minutes and reach for a cigarette. But twenty minutes passed and I was not yet craving a cigarette. I felt perhaps in another twenty minutes my weakness would win over. Still I had no craving. I was not convinced I could do without it much longer. So I sat there praying for the little girl. That was twenty-seven years ago and I never wanted to smoke again. But to God be the Glory, I knew that day that God had saved the little girl while he delivered me. I could only say, "Lord thou art God."

One day I came home to find my mother on the floor not able to get up. I managed to get her on the couch slowly. The next day the doctors told me to get her to the hospital. My daughter was working and my son was not there. In the meantime, I still had to open the hardware store and I had no one to fill in for me. I managed to get my mother in the car and to the hospital, but on the way there I was ridden with guilt about leaving her there and going to work. I told her I would be back after work. While I was driving I prayed the entire trip that God would ease her fear and give her perfect peace. Surely I knew she was afraid, mainly because she would be in a strange place and completely alone knowing absolutely no one on Long Island. When we reached the hospital they put her in a wheelchair and as we were going through the corridors, I heard someone say, "Hello Grandma." I heard my mother say "Hello Billy." I turned to see who it was. It was a young man in a doctor's uniform, who turned out to be one of the children that grew up on our block who my mother and I knew very well in Queens. To my surprise I asked him, "Billy, what are you doing here." He told me he was an X-Ray Technician in the hospital. He also said not to worry, he would watch out for her during the day. My mother was so happy... Jesus! Jesus! Jesus! I was on a cloud all the way to work that morning. I was praising God with my hands lifted and almost off the steering wheel all the way.

Casting all your cares upon Him, for He careth for you.

1 Peter 5:7

God's mercy is everlasting. When I returned that night to the hospital, I walked in the room to find my mother in a semi-coma. Doctors and nurse were there and they told me she developed an extremely high fever and they had tried everything they could, but the fever was not coming down. I knew that Jesus was a "doctor" in the sick room so I asked if there was a waiting room where I could go. They seemed a little taken back that I would leave the room at such at time as that, but I had to find a place where I could be alone with nobody around me, a place where I could pray and cry out to the Lord. It just didn't seem right that after all the Lord was doing in my new season and in my Mom's new season, that there would be a change of events so sudden that would cloud our joy. I don't know how long I stayed there in prayer but I finally got up and headed back to her room only to find her sitting up and smiling, talking and the nurse standing there with a stunned look on her face.

But thou, when thou prayest, enter into thy closet, and when thou hast shut thy door, pray to thy Father which is in secret; and thy Father which seeth in secret shall reward thee openly

Matthews 6:6

The nurse turned to me and said, "she suddenly opened her eyes and when they checked again the fever went back to normal." She added she had no explanation, but I smiled at her and said, "That's alright, I do." The next day I took her home from the hospital, and all she talked about was how the Lord brought her through even to the point of letting her walk again with ease.

I called my friend Virginia later on to tell her of all the things God was doing in my life, and how I bless the day she obeyed God and witnessed to me. I also spoke of my cousin Bobby who witnessed to me 9 years earlier, but then I did not listen. Virginia explained that Bobby planted the seed and was also obedient to God. She then told me that she knew I would be coming to the Lord. I asked her, "How could you possibly have known?" She reminded me of a time when I was at her house a few years earlier and came across a picture hanging on her kitchen wall. It was Jesus hanging on the cross with his arms up and the writing on it said, "I asked Jesus how much do you love me," and He answered, "this much" and "He died for me." When I saw it I carried on uncontrollably, then I asked her to take it down. "What!!?" I said, "Was bruised for my iniquities!!?" With tears in my eyes I said, "Virginia, how could you have something like that hanging on the wall?" She asked me why it bothered me so much, after all, seeing a crucifix around someone's neck or hanging in church surely never affected me like that before. But I said to her, "no, but what this is saying I don't want to hear or know!" She just smiled and took it down. Though I never asked her, I am sure she put it up again after I left and took it down when I was to come over. I am also sure that every time she passed by it on her wall she prayed fervently for me. Yes, Cousin Bobby planted the seed, Virginia watered it and God gave the increase.

Being raised in a Catholic Church, there was what is called "The Stations of the Cross." They were life size plaques of Jesus, and the different steps he took on the road to Calvary and we were to walk around the walls and stop at each one and say prayers using our Rosary beads. The prayers were not personal; we just repeated over and over the Hail Mary's and the Our Father's prayers. Nowhere did any of them say, "I loved you so much" or "I did this for you"; and there were twelve different plaques yet this one picture on Virginia's wall tore at my heart and pricked my spirit and humility filled my soul. Nowhere did I hear the voice of God speaking to me personally, but he was speaking, I just couldn't hear Him.

> *And when you pray, do not heap up empty phrases as the Gentiles do, for they think that they will be heard for their many words.*
>
> Matthews 6:7

My son had been arrested on drug charges and sentenced to two years in prison. At that time I learned of a prison ministry called "Cops for Christ." They were born again Christian police officers that ministered once a week at the prisons. I inquired about them and received a phone call from one of the officers, asking me where was my son imprisoned? He told me he was going there the next day; he prayed with me on the phone. I asked him if he knew what time he would be there and he said it had to be at 12 noon because he had to be somewhere later on. I thanked him and the next day while working, at noon, I went off to be by myself to pray. To my surprise, disbelief and confusion, I could not bring myself to utter a word. I stayed there till 1 p.m.; for a full hour I was in bewilderment asking God what was going on with me. I had overstayed my break too long, so I went back to work trying to somehow ignore my total confusion.

Three o'clock rolled around and suddenly in the presence of a group of unknowing employees, I began to sing out in a loud voice, "What a mighty God we serve, angels bow before Him, heaven and earth adore Him, what a mighty God we serve." There was a great sense of joy throughout the entire work area, but I still did not understand why I broke out with a song. At home that evening my son called me and mentioned a couple of men stopped in to visit Him that day and asked if I had sent them there. I admitted to him that I met them from the church and thought he would enjoy a visit. I then mentioned to him how I hoped his lunch didn't get cold (jokingly) since they came at noon, which was lunchtime. He answered, "Oh no mom, they weren't here at noon; they stopped in at 3 p.m. I almost dropped the phone from my hands because I could feel a mighty rushing wind passing by. Like "The man at the pool" Jesus just keeps showing up and showing up; when you least expect Him to. In the meantime God kept a promise and released me from the hardware store and blessed me with another job at a sweater factor, enabling me to attend Sunday services.

> *In His heart a man plans his course, but the Lord determines his steps.*
>
> Proverbs 16:9

This new job found me in an unfamiliar area about twenty miles from my home, which was also new to me. While driving home one night I found myself driving on Sunrise Highway with cars whizzing past me on both sides and speeding behind me; it was getting dark very early and I suddenly felt a freeze within me and I started to panic, but by now I was finding out too much about that man at the pool. With my hands clutching the steering wheel I cried out, "Jesus, Jesus." With that I calmed down, looked around and saw the car in front of me was now 2 car lengths ahead from me, the car behind me was also about 2 car lengths and the cars on both sides of me were nowhere to be seen. It remained that way until I reached my driveway some 10 miles later.

> *For I the Lord thy God will hold thy right hand, saying unto thee, Fear not, I will help thee.*
>
> Isaiah 41:13

In spite of the fact that my mom also loved the church, there was still the sense she was very lonely during the week, seeing no one. She was not able to go anywhere; since Long Island living to her was like living on a farm or in a desert. In my spirit I knew this was not of God. I started questioning God because daily the situation seemed to bother me more and more; therefore I put a fleece before the Lord, asking him to reveal his will and show me with a true conviction what I should do.

The next day was Saturday, and as usual I went to work. I came home from work at 12 noon as I always did on Saturdays; this time my mother expressed surprise that I was home early. I asked her why was she surprised, since I am always home at noon on Saturdays. With that, as I was going into another room, I heard my mother say to herself in a low voice, "I don't even know the difference of the days of the week anymore." I knew immediately that I had received my confirmation from the Lord. The next day, Sunday I drove to Queens, and by the grace of God, I managed to find a small two-room apartment in our old neighborhood where all her friends and family were. I came back and told her about the apartment. The look on her face will be in my memory always.

On my way to work the next day, I prayed and asked the Lord to make a way for me to explain to my employer that I would be leaving. I felt so bad and guilty of leaving mainly because he relied on me to manage the factory, which had about 20 employees at that time which dwindled down from about 50. As I walked in my employer met me at the door and asked me if I would first come into the office before going into the sweater department. He sat me down and in a very sad and in very apologetic tone of voice said, "Rose, the industry is taking a turn for the worse and after much deliberation, I have decided to shut down completely." He then added, "I cannot tell you how sorry I am, but I know I have no recourse." For a moment I stared at him, knowing God was making a way for me. God will make a way where there is no way. He started to apologize again, but I interrupted him and told him, "It's alright because God will take care of me and I know he will do the same for you, if you believe in Him." I spent that day and every day since, shouting Hallelujah Lord, now I surely know you were always there at the pool waiting for the right time to move.

> *See I am doing a new thing. Now it springs up ; do you not perceive it? I am making a way in the desert and streams in the waste land.*
>
> *Isaiah 43:19*

As I was making preparations to sell the house and move back to Queens, I developed severe pain in my side and found myself in the doctor's office. He put me through a series of tests and sent me home. Two days later he called me to his office; he found a problem with my kidneys. Before I returned to the doctor I first had to go to the altar. The Bible says, "Is any sick among you, let him call for the elders of the church and let them pray over him, anointing him with oil in the name of the Lord" (James 5:14) I knew this medical attack was a lie straight out of the pit of hell. I was told by my pastor to go back and demand the tests to be done again, which I did in spite of the doctor saying the first tests were very clear and evident. He called me two days later stuttering on the phone at a loss for words.

The 2nd test showed my kidneys were fine. But I gave him the right words to say, "Thank you Jesus."

I could not sell the house immediately and again God settled that matter. My daughter moved into the house and stayed there until I could sell it. We were back in Queens within a week, which couldn't be too soon for my mother. Already she was more alert and vibrant. Looking for a Pentecostal church, she was led to a church only a few blocks away. We went there that first Sunday and she never left it. It was a beautiful church and I was very happy for her. I on the other hand, did not feel fully fed there. A church may believe in sound doctrine, but if God has more for you, you will still be looking to satisfy your hunger and thirst.

In the meantime, I had to look for work. I prayed that God would again supply my needs and as I prayed I could hear the Lord say in my spirit, "look in the telephone directory and call the phone number that has more than one 7 in it. There was only one phone number and it had 2 consecutive 7's in it. I called the number and the man on the other end told me he just opened this sweater factory and needed desperately an experienced manager. I got the job and within 3 months I was earning top dollar. He was very satisfied and happy, so much so, he gave me the keys to open and close the shop. I used to go in an hour before the employees would come and sometimes I wouldn't see him for a whole day.

And my God will meet all your needs according to his glorious riches in Christ Jesus.
Philippians 4:19

One morning I came in as usual at 6 a.m. I would routinely go to the back door and raise an iron bar to prepare for truck deliveries. This one morning as I lifted the bar and began to walk away, the bar gave way and came down across my head. I started to bleed profusely above my eye. I grabbed some rags and pressed it on my eye. After about 30 minutes the bleeding stopped and I could see an open cut there, but I decided to not call the boss and went on with the day. At closing time he came to the shop and was shocked to see my face. He asked me why I did not call him immediately as he would have taken me to the doctor. I told him, I had no doubt God would see me through until I could get to a doctor.

The cut on my brow did open again and I did get three stitches but the Lord allowed me to get through the day and I testified of his goodness to all the employees and my employer. After that, even the atmosphere in the factory changed; every once in a while someone brought God into their conversation. The workplace became the most enjoyable place to work.

So whether you eat or drink or whatever you do, do all to the glory of God.
1Corinthians 10: 31

However, I still realized I had no church home. My mother was content praising the Lord where she was. I on the other hand was alternately going every other Sunday to the church on Long Island. I say every other Sunday because it was 70 miles away. On the alternate Sunday I would just attend another church, praying that I would find a church that I could be of one mind and one accord; a church where I could agree with its doctrine. After about one year, I discovered that I had never visited a church more than once. I also found it was becoming harder and harder to make that long trip, back and forth, to Long Island, especially since my job consisted of 60 hours a week including Saturdays.

I found myself becoming discouraged, yet determined in my spirit to have a church home. I did not want to become like the man at the pool getting too comfortable on my mat. Aware of this, I knew I had to let go and let God. I knew I was not going to find my church in the natural or looking at the physical. I knew that, up until then, everything that happened in my life was by the supernatural move of God. The only way I was going to find the right church, the church designed for my call and purpose was to sit down and reason with God and hand it all over to Him.

As I prayed, I reminded Him of how grateful and thankful I was of his goodness and mercy. I reminded him of my obedience bringing my mother back to Queens and thanked Him for blessing her with a church. I thanked him for blessing me with a job and for watching over me. Then I asked, "Now Lord, what about me? Surely you did not bring me here to leave me. Surely you meant it when you said, "I will give you the desires of your heart. Lord, if in my searching I am looking at the physical, forgive me. If I am overlooking your supernatural power, forgive me. But Lord, today

I give it all to you. No longer will I lead, starting today, I will follow." Suddenly, not even knowing God's plan, I was awe-struck with peace, joy and contentment; all this, after one year of running to different churches.

About three days later while working on a Saturday morning in the factory, two men and two women came at the door of the shop asking to purchase some sweaters at wholesale prices. I told them; yes we do sell to the public. I brought them over to the room where we kept the sweaters and they started to pick out numerous sweaters. I remarked that usually people would come in for one or two sweaters; I thought they were purchasing for a large family or families. One of the men said, "Oh, these sweaters are for the children in our church" (it was nearing Christmas). When I heard the word church I asked them what and where the church was and I expressed a desire to visit. They gladly invited me to the Friendly Church. With that we introduced ourselves to each other. First I was introduced to Mother Carol Nicholson, then Sister Annette Grant, then Deacon Hue Val Jones and last but not least was Pastor LeRoy Newman. I was elated just to be shaking the Pastor's hand. I went home that day and told my mother of the meeting at work and asked her if she would like to come that Sunday to visit the church. She came that Sunday. So what was the outcome of that Sunday's visit?

Let me just say this: all I did was open the church door and the Holy Ghost was there to greet me and I knew in an instant that God once again had answered my prayers supernaturally. I remember feeling God's presence so strongly that I wanted to go up to the front of the church. Before I could make up my mind to do so, suddenly Minister Frank Thompson walked up to us and introduced himself and asked if we would like to sit up front. I asked myself, "How much more was God going to move," I trembled to ask. By the way, Minister Frank Thompson is now Pastor Frank Thompson of Innerman Ministries. Before I left that day I met the Pastor's wife, Mother Mattie Newman, and their three sons, Emory, Tramain and Israel and so many others.

> *It is the spirit who gives life, the flesh is no help at all. The words that I have spoken to you are spirit and life.*
>
> *John 6:63*

You may ask why God took a whole year to bring me to my church. Well first, I was trying to do it on my own until I finally gave it all to him. Just because you are saved doesn't mean you tell God, ok Lord, thank you I'll take over now. But I do believe God looked at my faithfulness and persistence before He moved.

I came to meet Bishop's youngest son, Israel who was a young teenager at the time. He was such a well-mannered and polite child, which of course were all the children. I asked Bishop and Mother Newman if it would be all right for Israel to go with me one Sunday when I go to Long Island where I was in the habit of going every other week, alternatively, and visit my children. Little did I know I had my future pastor in my car. I enjoyed bringing him along, but eventually going out there and working long hours was getting very difficult for me, since it was seventy miles from Queens (140 miles round trip).

After a while daughter decided that she wanted to move; this led to me have to sell the house. I was able to use the money from the sale of the house to finally settle in and buy another home in Queens. Things were settling down. I had my church, a job, and a home in Queens and my mother was content. As I look back over these years, I can't help but to think of when I came back to Queens, I came back to a home, job and a church. "The wilderness can be a blessing." And I know that there is "a purpose in the wilderness."

My mother and I were in Queens about eight years when I discovered mom had Leukemia. The doctor had called one of my brothers and told him; but both of them expressed their wishes not to have my mother know. Uneasy over that, I reluctantly agreed with them, only not to upset them, but deep down inside I always felt she should have known. After all, she was also a praying woman. I prayed without ceasing for mom's healing; eventually I heard from God. He had other plans and I accepted his answer, "No." I see now that He healed her in a different way than I was praying for; but knowing of his mercy, I prayed that mom would never feel pain. To this prayer God answered, "Yes." If I didn't know anything about God then, what I learned about Him during my mother's last days has sustained me down through the years. Mom was being given chemo treatments in pill form, but she was told they were to strengthen her because she was very weak and losing weight. She accepted that, but I know her strength came from the Lord. Maybe she knew all along the circumstances, but she never said anything about it. There's one thing I know for sure, that every morning she would get up and sit at the kitchen table and read her Bible as soon as I left for work.

For I consider that the sufferings of this present time are not worth comparing with the glory that is to be revealed to us.

Romans 8:18

In February 1999, mother was hospitalized, and I was told she had only about 3 months to live. My mom was not told this, but as I stood at her bedside she cried out to me desperately, "RoRo, take me home today please." I told her that the doctors would like for her to stay a little longer, till she felt stronger, but she cried out again, "no, no, today please." I cannot explain the pain in my heart, but I didn't realize at the time that the Lord was speaking to her.

I have fought a good fight, I have finished my course, I have kept the faith.

2 Timothy 4:7

Mom came home that afternoon by ambulance with a hospital bed that was set up in the living room. That night, my uncle (my mother's brother) came to see her. My mother motioned to him to come near her. He had to bend down close to her because she couldn't speak loudly. She said something to him and he walked away laughing. I asked him, "What did she say?" He answered, "Oh you know your mother, always saying things that make no sense. She told me she's going to a wedding." The Holy Ghost immediately directed me to what was happening. You see, as I mentioned earlier in this book, my mom was struck as a child with spinal meningitis, which left her unable to fully be able to explain the ways of the world. But my uncle who as I mentioned earlier in the book was an extremely intelligent man, so much so, that he would speak on Einstein, Nostradamus and other masterminds missed the point. "Eyes have not seen, ear have not heard." Mom was getting ready to go home. Yes, she wanted to be home to go home. The next day the Lord called mom home, God does answer prayers. Mom suffered no pain up until that day.

During the course of the next three months, I found myself staying in the house thanking God for answered prayers, but at the same time I missed mother and felt all alone. Mom and I didn't agree at times on a lot of things and one of which was family matters, but we both went through, no matter what. I spent those next three months, mostly in solitary confinement constantly asking Jesus to lessen the burden.

One day as I sat in my living room, it had been the third day of constant rain. So much so, when I looked out, I could see the ground so soft from the rain, one needed to wear boots because of the mud. There was not a soul anywhere to be seen in the streets; at that moment I was moved to pay a visit to the cemetery. After wrestling with myself and reasoning with the Lord, I concluded that it wasn't a day to go to the cemetery. But I got dressed anyway and got in my car. On the way, I stopped to buy a plant to put at her graveside. I still could not understand why God prompted me to visit the grave in this drenching downpour. I even had the audacity to tell Him … "After all, Lord, she's not there, she's with you." It was still pouring rain as I took the plant out of the car to the grave. It was then I realized that I had not brought a shovel to dig up the soil. But the ground was so saturated I decided I would use my hands to dig. After I planted the flowers, I stood up, stared for a while, and suddenly began dancing and praising God for his goodness and ever present help in the time of need. I let out a loud scream thanking Him, but asking Him, "What about me?" I don't know how long I remained there; all I knew was that there was an outpouring of the Holy Ghost, and my feeling that God was not through with me yet. Like the man at the pool, he didn't send for Jesus, He just showed up; except this time I didn't need anyone to put me in the pool. I was already completely wet from "a latter rain." I don't know how long I danced around the grave; even so, I don't know how long David danced either. Surely I danced until I heard him say, "I will never leave you nor forsake you."

> *You have kept count of my tossings, put my tears in your bottle, are they not in your book?*
>
> *Psalm 56:8*

As I started walking back to the car, I realized my hands were completely covered with mud. There were faucets on the ground, so I went over to the first one and opened it, only to find no water would come out. Not giving it much thought I walked about 40 feet away to the next one. That one was also dry. I walked over in the opposite direction over to the next faucet and again there was no water. I decided, in spite of it all, I would have no choice but to drive home with mud on my hands and the steering wheel. As I started to walk towards the car, I suddenly heard the sound of water gushing loudly. Turning around I could see water not just dripping from the faucets but rushing out fiercely. I ran over and washed my hands. I cannot recall whether the water stopped immediately after I washed my hands or not; all I know is that I went home that day a different person than I was when I went to the grave site. The experience was so awesome, I started to go back again because I could not forget what the Lord had done for me that day; this was only the beginning of my new joy in the Lord.

> You are the God who works wonders, you have made known your might among the peoples.
>
> *Psalm 77:14*

A few days later I was sharing my story with friends who were more familiar with that cemetery than I was. They seemed to doubt that what I was telling them was true. When I asked them why, they told me that the faucets in the cemetery were all shut down from November to June. I was there the last week of April. Well it's not important whether or not they believed my story because that wasn't the end of the story; it was only the beginning of my continued deliverance and commitment to my visionary purpose. I speak as someone who God has delivered from the occult and put upon me the cloak of His supernatural power. During the past years I have spent my days testifying of the goodness of Jesus and all he has done for me. God brought me into a new season; a season of witnessing to a world of which I am not a part. "I'm in the world but not of the world, in the flesh but not of the flesh." God has blessed me to witness in nursing homes and in assisted living residences. I have started a home Bible study in my neighborhood. I thank God for turning my life around from what man meant for evil to what God intended for good.

If we confess our sins, He is faithful and just to forgive us our sins and to cleanse us from all unrighteousness.

1 John 1:9

If you break a mirror and it shatters into a thousand pieces and you cannot put it back together, you can still look at the pieces and see a reflection. The man at the pool of Bethesda when he was able to reach poolside could see a reflection of himself as he is but not as he was. In your mind's eye you can see where God has brought you from and like the man at the pool, give God the glory. Sometimes I can almost see Him standing by my side.

As I said earlier in the beginning of the book, I found it hard to sit down and write, mainly because it depressed me. When I mentioned this to my Bishop, in his wisdom, he said nothing. "There is a time to speak; there is a time to be quiet." His silence was deafening, yet at the same time saying, "depression is not of God."

There were other times during the two years of writing; Satan would try to convince me that I was exposing my life for everyone to see. However God intervened through the Holy Ghost and said, "the only ones that will be exposed would be those with blinded eyes and pointing fingers."

Three week before this book was finished I overheard a question… "What are the two most important days of your life?" The answer was… "The day I was born and the day I found out why." At the time I heard it I thought it to be a fascinating answer and just left it at that. But yesterday I finished my book and this morning, no sooner than I opened my eyes I received a revelation from the Lord, "Now you know why." No, my dear brothers and sisters, I'm still not all that I should be, I'm not all I could be, but I thank God I'm not where I used to be. There is one thing I know, and all my energies are directed on this one thing: Forgetting the past and looking forward to what lies ahead.

I wrote this book with one purpose in mind, to give God the glory for what He has done in my life. Midway, I knew this would serve as a testimony to others. God heals in many different ways. By the time I finished this book, I discovered I was completely healed of looking in the rearview mirror.

So when you see me, please don't ask me where my mat is…. I no longer need it. It will only get in my way while I am lifting holy hands to the Lord. You see, I was 38 years at the pool (literally), and not a day more….

The man at the pool lay there with an illness he bore for thirty-eight years; he laid there on a mat as his bed. They tell me that his mat was to make him comfortable. I too, in my state of denial, had a mat for thirty-eight years; but I heard Jesus speak to me through His Word, "I will send you a comforter," so why would I need a mat?

Mats can be used to wipe one's feet clean, but Jesus said to me, not only will I make your feet clean, "I'll make you (your whole body) white as snow," so why would I need a mat?

I have seen mats in the 99-cent stores, easy access, but you get what you pay for, and they don't last very long. Jesus told me, "My mercy endureth forever." Why did I waste 38 years I ask myself, "was it a waste?" If it were not for those 38 years this book would not have been written; or was it because He knew that during the 39th year I would consider giving up? Only God knows. As He has always done, He came into my life right on time. At the pool, I didn't recognize Jesus for who He was, but that doesn't mean he never showed up.

I didn't recognize Him because I was too busy with "self." But even when "self" was threatening to take control of my life during the 38th year of my denial, He was right there to step in right on time, and say to me "take up thy bed."

As I look back over those 38 years, I can see the plan that God had to transform me, but I had to first become a new creature by the renewing of my mind. Now I need no one to put me in the pool, neither do I need the comfort of the mat.

For…

I am saved, sanctified, and filled with the Holy Ghost; I can tell the world about this, I can tell the nation I'm blessed, tell them what the Lord has done, and that the comforter has come, and it brought joy, unspeakable joy to my soul.

Printed in the United States
By Bookmasters